PATHWISE® School Leaders

Transform School Leaders into Instructional Leaders

Help new and experienced supervisors, principals, and superintendents acquire the knowledge and skills they need to become instructional leaders with three research-based PATHWISE products.

School Leadership Development

Materials, training, and professional development to help school leaders:

- Incorporate the ISLLC Standards for School Leaders into their professional practice
- Measure performance levels against national standards
- Develop their skill at identifying and correcting issues

Data-driven School Improvement Series

Workbooks and training that:

- Create a framework for collecting and assessing data
- Demonstrate how data can drive school improvement and help meet NCLB challenges
- Provide practical suggestions for improvement efforts at the classroom level

Framework Observation Program

A comprehensive professional development program focusing on observer training that:

- Teaches how to analyze critical differences in levels of performance
- Trains school leaders in observation techniques that improve school performance
- Provides consistant observation criteria and levels of performance for both teachers and observers

Start your transition to instructional leadership today

To learn more about these and other PATHWISE Professional Development products and services, call **1-800-297-9051** or visit **www.ets.org/pathwise**.

(ETS®)

Pathwise.

istening.
Learning.
Leading.

Educational Testing Service

A FRAMEWORK FOR SCHOOL LEADERS:

LINKING THE ISLLC STANDARDS TO PRACTICE

KAREN HESSEL

JOHN HOLLOWAY

PEARSON

Merrill
Prentice Hall

Upper Saddle River, New Jersey
Columbus, Ohio

Educational Testing Service (ETS), headquartered in Princeton, New Jersey, is the world's largest private educational testing and measurement organization and a leader in educational research. A nonprofit company, ETS is dedicated to serving the needs of individuals, educational institutions and agencies, and governmental bodies in 181 countries.

ETS's Teaching and Learning Division is committed to supporting learning and advancing good teaching through a coherent approach to licensing, advanced certification, and professional development for teachers and school leaders.

In response to the national movement towards standards-based education and assessment, the division is collaborating with national organizations, states, school districts, and accomplished practicing teachers and administrators to develop exemplary, research-based professional development products and services for educators.

Included are the PATHWISE® Framework Induction Program for beginning teachers, the PATHWISE Framework Leader Academy, the PATHWISE Framework Observation System, the PATHWISE Framework Portfolio Program for experienced teachers, the PATHWISE Teacher Evaluation System, Assessment Wizard, and the PATHWISE School Leaders Series.

For more information, visit www.teachingandlearning.org.

Educational Testing Service
MS 18-D
Rosedale Road
Princeton, NJ 08541-0001
Web site: http://www.ets.org/pathwise

Vice President and Executive Publisher: Jeffery W. Johnston
Executive Editor: Debra A. Stollenwerk
Director of Marketing: Ann Castel Davis
Marketing Manager: Darcy Betts Prybella
Marketing Coordinator: Brian Mounts

This book was printed and bound by Courier Kendallville, Inc. The cover was printed by Phoenix Color Corp.

10 9 8 7 6 5 4 3 2 1
ISBN: 0-13-172396-0

TABLE OF CONTENTS

LIST OF FIGURES

ABOUT THE AUTHORS

Karen Hessel is the Principal in Residence at Educational Testing Service (ETS®), located in Princeton, New Jersey. As Principal in Residence, Karen's main duties include design of professional development programs in the area of new teacher induction as well as the Leadership Series for school administrators. Prior to coming to ETS, Karen served as a middle school science teacher, district developer and supervisor of gifted and talented programs K-12, and for the past 15 years as a nationally recognized Blue Ribbon School principal. In addition, Karen is an ETS-certified national trainer for all PATHWISE® Professional Development Programs.

John Holloway is the project director for the School Leadership Series of licensure assessment in the Teaching and Learning Division at ETS. As project director, his main duties include test development and assisting states throughout the country in the adoption and implementation of the licensure series. Prior to joining ETS, John served as a high school science teacher for several years and then a high school principal for 25 years. In addition, John was an adjunct professor, teaching graduate courses in school leadership and administration.

Dear Reader,

A recent article depicted the Superman mystique in placing the following advertisement for a school principal position:

"Must be more powerful than a locomotive, faster than a speeding bullet, able to leap tall buildings in a single bound—blue uniform with tights and cape furnished."

This insightful description of the role of a principal is, at a first blush, humorous. The description, however, does depict reality when one considers the myriad and diverse roles and responsibilities of the principal and the exhausting demand on time for those who function in the role. Our schools find themselves not only educating but also often caring for the additional needs of every child who crosses the threshold. As this era of high academic standards, testing, and accountability stretches before us, the principal's basic responsibilities are shifting dramatically. Now, it's agreed that the principal is—should be, must be—in charge of learning. Traditional management and discipline duties, however, have not disappeared. Extraordinary demands have been placed on principals today making their jobs in many instances simply not doable.

In 1994, the National Association of Elementary School Principals (NAESP) and the National Association of Secondary School Principals (NASSP) were part of a consortium formed to develop a set of standards to define and guide the practice of school leaders. The Interstate School Leaders Licensure Consortium (ISLLC) produced the ISLLC Standards for School Leaders in 1996. These standards are not meant to be all-inclusive, but are focused on indicators of knowledge, dispositions, and performances that are important to effective school leadership. *A Framework for School Leaders: Linking the ISLLC Standards to Practice* focuses on the ISLLC Standards and, through the use of rubrics, seeks to provide meaningful descriptions of professional practice. The common language for redefining and focusing the role of school leaders as defined in the framework can help school leaders articulate their role, and can serve as a standards-based approach to describe various school leaders' levels of performance.

It is our hope that *A Framework for School Leaders: Linking the ISLLC Standards to Practice* will help principals and superintendents throughout America find ways to help school leaders be more effective in their roles.

<table>
<tr><td>Vincent L. Ferrandino</td><td>Gerald N. Tirozzi</td></tr>
<tr><td>Executive Director</td><td>Executive Director</td></tr>
<tr><td>NAESP</td><td>NASSP</td></tr>
</table>

National Association of Elementary School Principals

The 28,500 members of the National Association of Elementary School Principals (NAESP) provide administrative and instructional leadership for public and private elementary and middle schools throughout the United States, Canada, and overseas. Founded in 1921, NAESP is today a vigorously independent, professional association with its own headquarters in Alexandria, Virginia, just across the Potomac River from the nation's capital. From this special vantage point, NAESP conveys the unique perspective of the elementary and middle school principal to the highest policy councils of our national government. Through national and regional meetings, award-winning publications, and joint efforts with its 50 state affiliates, NAESP is a strong advocate both for its members and for the 33 million American children enrolled in preschool, kindergarten, and grades 1 through 8. NAESP offers a wide array of professional development opportunities and resources, including its newest standards publication, *Leading Quality Learning Communities: What Principals Should Know and Be Able to Do.*

1615 Duke Street, Alexandria, VA 22314-3483. Phone (703) 684-3345.
Fax: (703) 549-5568. E-mail: naesp@naesp.org. Web site: www.naesp.org.

National Association of Secondary School Principals

The National Association of Secondary School Principals (NASSP) is the preeminent organization of middle level and high school principals, assistant principals, and aspiring school leaders. NASSP promotes improvement of secondary education and the role of school leaders by advocating high professional and academic standards, addressing the challenges facing school leaders, providing a "national voice," building public confidence in education, and strengthening the role of the principal as instructional leader.

Recognizing that successful schools require leaders who are able to perform at optimum levels and who have the knowledge and skills necessary to meet present and future challenges, NASSP's Office of Leadership Development and Assessment offers a variety of assessment and development programs designed to identify and develop leadership talent.

NASSP works with school districts, regional service agencies, boards of cooperative services, universities, professional associations, state departments of education, and other providers of programs and services to establish assessment/development centers. These centers provide local facilitators with the knowledge, skill, and support to deliver NASSP professional skill development or assessment programs that meet the needs of all school leaders.

National Association of Secondary School Principals, 1904 Association Drive, Reston, VA 20191-1537. Phone: (703) 860-0200. Fax: (703) 476-5432. Web site: www.principals.org.

PREFACE

Several years ago, Bill was a high school teacher with ten years experience. He also received a license from the state to serve as a building principal. Three years of attending graduate school in the evening and on weekends prepared Bill for this possible new career in education. In these courses Bill learned about the issues school leaders would face and began to develop some understanding of how they might be confronted. He learned about curriculum planning and development, teacher evaluation and improvement, budget and finance, school law, and all those other skills needed to ensure successful leadership. At the end of one school day Bill attended a faculty meeting called by his principal. There was only one item on the meeting agenda that day, an announcement that the school would be selecting a new assistant principal and this new person would begin the job within two weeks. At the meeting, the principal made the announcement and made it perfectly clear that he was looking for only one skill in this new leader. As he put it, "I'm only looking for a 'head knocker,' someone who will be tough on kids. Don't think you'll be doing any curriculum, budget, or scheduling." Bill went home after the meeting and considered applying for the job. The next morning he gave the principal his completed application and within two weeks was out of the classroom and into his new duties as assistant principal. Bill soon learned that the principal was not kidding about the nature of the job. Virtually every day, all day, Bill dealt with discipline problems and teacher and parent complaints. And, this continued unabated for several years. Bill often thought, "Why was I trained to do curriculum and to help teachers grow and students learn, when my job has nothing to do with these important responsibilities? When do we lead?"

Far too often, Bill's administrative experience has been the norm in most school buildings. While these duties are important, the times are changing. A powerful force in bringing about the way we think about school leadership started in 1994, when the Council of Chief State School Officers (CCSSO) formed the Interstate School Leaders Licensure Consortium (ISLLC). ISLLC was charged with collaborating with the national professional organizations representing school leaders, including the National Association of Elementary School Principals (NAESP) and the National Association of Secondary School Principals (NASSP) with creating a new set of standards to define and guide the practice of school leaders. These Standards, now known as the *ISLLC Standards for School Leaders*, created in 1996, have become a driving force in the way school leadership should and will be viewed. These Standards are not all-inclusive, but do focus on those indicators of knowledge, dispositions, and performances that are most important to effective school leadership — a focus on teaching and learning and a concern for the success for all students. The intellectual architecture that supports the Standards has been thoroughly researched and documented and is summarized in Appendix A of this book. This framework for school leaders addresses only the ISLLC Standards and seeks to link these Standards to professional practice in a meaningful and descriptive way. Readers are certainly invited and encouraged to go beyond these Standards and this framework in reflecting on their own practice and craft a model that works best for them by considering other standards that might exist. However, for effective school leadership, it is our belief and the belief of experts throughout the field, that the ISLLC Standards must form the very core and foundation of the leader's professional practice.

The organization of this book is somewhat linear and sequential. We start with a basic description of what is meant by a framework. Joe Murphy and Neil Shipman then discuss the creation of the ISLLC Standards and the impact they are having on school leadership. Next, we attempt to put school leadership in an historical context, by describing its genesis and evolution. Some background material that defines the vocabulary and principles that underlie the construct of the framework follows this brief history of leadership. Chapter 6 is the actual framework for school leaders, consisting of its 24 Component Performance Tables and related descriptive text. Finally, Chapter 7 gives the reader some insight about what must be considered in actually applying the framework to practice.

ACKNOWLEDGMENTS

In the completion of this book, we would like to express our sincerest appreciation to Educational Testing Service for giving us the opportunity to become involved in this exciting project, designed to advance school leadership. Many individuals supported our efforts; most significantly, however, we must recognize Mari Pearlman, Vice President of the ETS Teaching and Learning Division, who provided the inspiration for the project. Cindy Tocci, director of the ETS Teaching and Learning Division professional development group guided the work, and Charlotte Danielson, also of ETS, provided the intellectual stimulus to start us thinking about a framework for school leaders. Rick Tannenbaum, ETS Teaching and Learning Division director of research, provided invaluable assistance in describing some of the more technical aspects of the book. In addition, there would be no framework without the initial research and work done by Joe Murphy and Neil Shipman, who also supported and guided our efforts. Finally, Bill Thomas, and his wife Marge, proved invaluable in guiding our writing, keeping our thoughts focused on the task, and being cheerleaders for the project.

Several other individuals and groups played a vital role in the creation of the framework. These included:

- Our first local focus team of school leaders—Doug Bohrer, Joyce Maso, Helen Pappas, and Diane Schmidt

- Katherine Bartlett, Tracey Dwight, Lynne Heilman and Gina Page who provided support services

- Karlene Farquharson and Ilene Skolnik who helped edit the draft manuscript

- Karen McQuillen, Educational Testing Service librarian, and Dr. Dennis Buss of Rider University, who assisted us with the research

- Professor Patrick Allen, from Union College, who gave us initial advice, feedback, and encouragement

■ Salli Long, our editorial project manager, and the ETS Publications Department Staff

■ The Delaware Principals Association; the Dubuque, Iowa Community Schools Administrative team; and principals from the Philadelphia, Pennsylvania school system for their efforts in providing valuable feedback during the final phase of the project

■ The principals, superintendents, and professors from around the country who have experience using the Standards in their practice and who contributed to the framework by providing us their own personal views about the meaning of the Standards. These good friends include LaVerne B. Allen, Michael "Mick" Arnold, Francis V. Barnes, JoAnn Bartoletti, Patrick A. Bashaw, Douglas J. Bohrer, Robert Buchanan, Tom Clark, Elaine Peeler Davis, Rudy Duran, Noel T. Farmer, Jeanne Fiene, Jo Fyfe, Geoffrey R. Geiger, Clarence Golden, Jack Herlihy, Dwight Luckett, James R. McGowan, Earl F. Newby, Margaret Pavol, Dolores Stegner, Jack Walsh, and John Williams

We are deeply indebted to the National Association of Elementary School Principals and the National Association of Secondary School Principals. These two organizations were directly instrumental in providing us the guidance, support, and inspiration in undertaking this project. Because of their leadership and vision, we proudly offer this framework to our colleagues, all school leaders and their communities.

Finally, we are deeply indebted to our professional colleagues, both teachers and fellow administrators, with whom we have had the pleasure of working over the many years as school principals. But, most importantly, we express deepest gratitude to all the students who attended our schools, delighted and inspired us, and helped mold our vision about what is most important about public education — teaching and learning and the success of the students.

A FRAMEWORK FOR SCHOOL LEADERS:

LINKING THE ISLLC STANDARDS TO PRACTICE

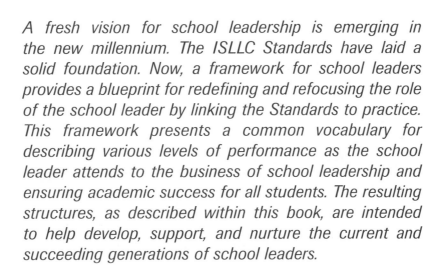

A fresh vision for school leadership is emerging in the new millennium. The ISLLC Standards have laid a solid foundation. Now, a framework for school leaders provides a blueprint for redefining and refocusing the role of the school leader by linking the Standards to practice. This framework presents a common vocabulary for describing various levels of performance as the school leader attends to the business of school leadership and ensuring academic success for all students. The resulting structures, as described within this book, are intended to help develop, support, and nurture the current and succeeding generations of school leaders.

INTRODUCTION TO THE FRAMEWORK FOR SCHOOL LEADERS

Since the publication of *Enhancing Professional Practice: A Framework for Teaching* (Danielson, 1996) educators have discovered the value of a clear and research-based definition of good teaching, one that respects its complexity and multiple demands. The framework has offered teachers, and the administrators who work with them, a "roadmap to the territory" of teaching, and a guide for novices just entering the profession, and a structure for experienced teachers improving their practice.

A Framework for School Leaders: Linking the ISLLC Standards to Practice offers the same advantages for site and district administrators. This framework for school leaders is organized around the core proposition that the most critical aspect of a school leader's work is the continuous improvement of student learning. All of the other multiple tasks and activities are in the service of that core responsibility. Providing leadership and vision, marshalling the talents and experience of the professional staff and volunteers, managing budgets and coordinating schedules, keeping the building in good repair—all of these are in support of the school's primary function: high-level student learning.

School principals, superintendents, and other school leaders are confronted with the daunting task of providing structure and coherence to the school's instructional mission while simultaneously responding to the sometimes intense pressure from parents, the community, and even the district's own central administration. Small wonder that the daily work of students and teachers in classrooms is sometimes left in the dust.

The framework for school leaders is based on the standards published by the Council of Chief State School Officers (CCSSO) in 1996. They were created by the Interstate School Leaders Licensure Consortium (ISLLC), a project of the CCSSO, and were intended to offer coherence and structure to the complex work of school leaders, at all levels of the organization. Thus, they apply to superintendents as well as site administrators.

The great contribution of this book is that it translates these somewhat global standards to the specific responsibilities of school leaders.

Just as the framework for teaching may be used for any number of purposes, so may the framework for school leaders.

Preparation of the next generation of administrators. Institutions that prepare school leaders will find the framework invaluable in structuring their course offerings as well as their clinical experiences. They will find this framework invaluable as a guide for the organization and the structure of their programs.

Mentoring of new administrators. As new administrators first take on the sometimes overwhelming task of running a school, of being the place where the buck stops, they will find the framework extremely useful to provide guidance for their work. They will also discover that the framework can help them keep the different aspects of their role in perspective, to see the many, and immediate, demands placed on them in the service of the school's instructional mission.

Professional development of practicing administrators. As experienced administrators constantly seek to improve their practice, they will discover that the framework for school leaders can offer guidance as to where to put their efforts. Through self-assessment, goal-setting, and self-directed professional inquiry, administrators can discover where their greatest needs lie and can plan accordingly.

Administrator evaluation. In these days of increased accountability for all educators, the school district owes its public a coherent and comprehensive system of administrator evaluation. Are all administrators performing well in their roles? Does the district have a systematic method by which it can even answer that question, and does it have an approach to helping individuals remedy any weaknesses that emerge? The framework for school leaders can provide a foundation for developing such a system of evaluation.

The framework for school leaders represents a significant contribution to the field, a "blueprint" for the complex work of school administration that properly situates all of the myriad tasks and duties within the core instructional mission of the school. This blueprint will serve, in the years ahead, as the foundation of professional preparation and professional learning.

THE INTERSTATE SCHOOL LEADERS LICENSURE CONSORTIUM (ISLLC) STORY: A BRIEF NARRATIVE

by Joseph Murphy & Neil J. Shipman

Organization and Mission

Formed in 1994, the Interstate School Leaders Licensure Consortium is a collection of many of the major parties with a stake in educational leadership; these include the states (currently 30), the relevant professional associations (e.g., NASSP, NAESP, AASA), and the universities (e.g., NCPEA, AACTE, UCEA).

Under the auspices of the Council of Chief State School Officers (CCSSO) (where our sister organization, the Interstate New Teachers Assessment and Support Consortium [INTASC], is housed) and in cooperation with the National Policy Board for Educational Administration, ISLLC set out to develop a powerful framework for redefining school leadership and to connect that framework to strategies for improving educational leadership throughout the nation. Our work, therefore, has been in the service of rebuilding or reculturing the leadership infrastructure of schooling.

Beginning with Standards

Many strategies are being used to upgrade the quality of leadership in the educational arena. The ISLLC team decided at the outset of our work, however, to focus on standards. This strategy made sense for several reasons. First, based on the work on standards in other arenas of educational reform, especially the efforts of INTASC, we were convinced that standards provided an especially appropriate point for reform. Second, we found a major void in this area of educational administration — a set of common standards was conspicuous by its absence. Finally, we believed that the standards approach provided the best avenue to allow diverse stakeholders to drive improvement efforts along a variety of fronts — licensure, program approval, candidate assessment, and so forth.

Within that framework, we began work on a common set of Standards that would apply to nearly all formal leadership positions in education, not just the principalship. We acknowledge full well that there are differences in leadership that correspond to roles, but ISLLC members were unanimous in their belief that the central aspects of the role are the same for all school leadership positions.

While recognizing the full range of responsibilities of school leaders, we decided to focus on those topics that formed the heart and soul of effective leadership. This decision led us in two directions. First, because we did not want to lose the key issues in a forest of standards, we deliberately framed a parsimonious model at the standard level. Thus, we produced only six Standards. Second, we continually centered on matters of learning and teaching and the creation of powerful learning environments. Not only do several Standards directly highlight learning and teaching, but also all the Standards take on meaning to the extent that they support a learning environment. Throughout, the success of students is paramount. The ISLLC Standards marry leadership to learning, management with measurement of academic growth, and stewardship to the development of productive learning communities.

ISLLC's Intellectual Architecture

The Consortium tackled the design strategy in three ways. First, we relied heavily on the research on the linkages between educational leadership and productive schools, especially in terms of outcomes for children and youth. Our focus was on schools that: (a) had high levels of student performance, (b) could demonstrate that learning was equitably distributed across the student population, and (c) could take credit for the value added in learning.

Second, we sought out significant trends in society and education that hold implications for emerging views of leadership—and subsequently for the Standards that give meaning to those new perspectives on leadership. Looking to the larger society that envelopes schooling, the Consortium identified a handful of powerful dynamics that will likely shape the future of education and, perforce, the types of leadership required for tomorrow's schools. To begin with, our vision of education is influenced by the knowledge that the social fabric of society is changing, often in dramatic ways. On the one hand, the pattern of the fabric is being rewoven. In particular, we are becoming a more diverse society— racially, linguistically and culturally. On the other hand, the social fabric is unraveling for many children and their families. Poverty is increasing. Indexes of physical, mental, and moral well-being are declining. The stock of social capital is decreasing as well.

The perspective of the Consortium on schooling and leadership is also colored by the knowledge that the economic foundations of society are being recast as well. The shift to a post-industrial society, the advance of the global marketplace, the increasing reliance on technology, and a growing infatuation with market-based solutions to social needs pose significant new challenges for education. We believe that these challenges will require new types of leadership in schools.

Third, turning to schooling itself, Consortium members distilled three central changes, all of which augur well for a redefined portfolio of leadership skills for school administrators. On one level, we are struggling to redefine learning and teaching to more successfully challenge and engage all youngsters in the education process. Educators are rethinking long-prevailing views of knowledge, intelligence, assessment, and instruction. On a second level, we are hearing strong rumblings that community-focused and caring-centered conceptions of schooling will increasingly compete for legitimacy with more established notions of school organizations as hierarchies and bureaucracies. Finally, stakeholders external to the building — parents, interested members of the corporate sector, and leaders in the community — will increasingly play significantly enhanced roles in education.

The ISLLC Standards are scaffolded on the knowledge base that connects the work of school leaders (principals, superintendents, and others) to more effective organizational performance, especially student learning outcomes. The empirical knowledge base is laid out in the writings of the Chair of ISLLC, all of which pre-date the release of the Standards. Readers who desire more detailed information on the studies that support the Standards are directed to the references in the articles, chapters, and books listed in Appendix A, at the end of this book. Furthermore, recent empirical work in the support of the Standards can be reviewed in Murphy, et al (2001), *The Productive High School*, Newbury Park, CA: Corwin Press.

Framing Principles

In addition to its intellectual foundations, the Standards were also formed by reference to a set of guiding principles. At the outset of the project, it became clear that our work would be strengthened considerably if we could craft a set of overarching values to guide our efforts. Over time, we saw that these principles actually could serve two functions. First, they acted as a touchstone to which we regularly returned to test the scope and focus of emerging products. Second, they helped give meaning to the Standards and indicators. The following seven principles helped orient all of our work:

- Standards should reflect the centrality of student learning.

- Standards should acknowledge the changing role of school leadership.

- Standards should recognize the collaborative nature of school leadership.

- Standards should be high, upgrading the quality of the profession.

- Standards should inform performance-based systems of assessment and evaluation for school leaders.

- Standards should be integrated and coherent.

- Standards should be predicated on the concepts of access, opportunity, and empowerment for all members of the school community.

ISLLC Standards

The ISLLC Standards are presented and unpacked in considerable detail in this volume. As a type of foreshadowing, they are listed more succinctly below.

STANDARD

A school administrator is an educational leader who promotes the success of all students by facilitating the development, articulation, implementation, and stewardship of a vision of learning that is shared and supported by the school community.

STANDARD

A school administrator is an educational leader who promotes the success of all students by advocating, nurturing, and sustaining a school culture and instructional program conducive to student learning and staff professional growth.

STANDARD

A school administrator is an educational leader who promotes the success of all students by ensuring management of the organization, operations, and resources for a safe, efficient, and effective learning environment.

STANDARD

A school administrator is an educational leader who promotes the success of all students by collaborating with families and community members, responding to diverse community interests and needs, and mobilizing community resources.

STANDARD

A school administrator is an educational leader who promotes the success of all students by acting with integrity, with fairness, and in an ethical manner.

STANDARD

A school administrator is an educational leader who promotes the success of all students by understanding, responding to, and influencing the larger political, social, economic, legal, and cultural contexts.

In most ways, the Standards speak for themselves. What are missing in this abbreviated list, however, are the roughly 200 indicators that help define the Standards. Indicators are clustered under three headings for each Standard — knowledge, dispositions, and performances.

The ISLLC Standards at Work

As we noted earlier, the Standards were developed with an eye on reculturing the profession of school administration—on both its academic and practice axes—for example, by improving the quality of programs that prepare school leaders and ensuring greater accountability for the efforts of these school leaders; by creating a framework to better assess candidates for licensure and relicensure; and by establishing a foundation on which certification programs can be constructed. They were designed to be used by individual educators, schools, school districts, state agencies, and professional associations. To date, we are seeing evidence that the Standards are being employed in a variety of ways—examples of which are provided below.

Standards development. A number of states and professional associations are using the ISLLC framework to develop their own standards. In some cases (e.g., Illinois, Ohio, Kentucky, and the New Jersey Principals and Supervisors Association), the ISLLC Standards have been adopted *whole cloth*. In other places (e.g., Louisiana, the Texas Superintendents Association, and the Board of Education of the City of New York), they have served as the raw material from which model standards were created. Similar development and benchmarking work is underway in a variety of other venues (e.g., Iowa's Professional Standards Board—the Iowa Board of Educational Examiners).

District and association-based new leaders' academies. States, school districts, and professional associations are sometimes using the Standards to help develop programs to identify and nurture the development of potential school leaders. For example, the Alabama Council of School Administration and Supervision has grounded its new professional development program for prospective school site leaders on the ISLLC Standards.

Principal evaluation. A number of districts (e.g., Hilliard, Ohio, and Highland Park, Illinois) and states like West Virginia and Delaware are using the Standards as an evaluative template for school principals.

Preparation program redesign. Considerable energy is being devoted to linking the ISLLC Standards to the reform of formal training programs for school administrators. These efforts run the gamut from individual universities (e.g., Central Arkansas State University), to cooperative cross-university activities (e.g., Missouri Professors' Association), to whole-state reform initiatives (e.g., North Carolina, Maryland, Mississippi, and Louisiana).

Program accreditation. A number of states (e.g., North Carolina) are framing their reviews of preparation programs on the ISLLC Standards. Other states (e.g., Mississippi) are beginning to link program accreditation with passing rates of students taking the new interstate licensure examination for school leaders — which we describe more fully below. In addition, the NCATE review process for preparation programs is soon to be scaffolded on the ISLLC Standards.

Professional development. States (e.g., Ohio and Rhode Island) and professional associations (e.g., Illinois Elementary Principals Association) are also bringing the ISLLC Standards to bear on the continuing education of school leaders. School districts, such as the District of Columbia, also are anchoring professional development of administrators to the Standards. In addition, through the Consortium, 30 states and all the major, relevant professional associations have created two Standards-based portfolios for professional development.

Relicensure. A few states anticipate using the portfolio instruments noted above under professional development to relicense principals.

Certification. The National Policy Board for Educational Administration (NPBEA) — including the three professional associations with the closest links to administrative practice (AASA, NAESP, and NASSP) — have opened discussions about developing a system of professional certification for leaders. The ISLLC Standards form part of the platform they plan to use in constructing the certification system.

Licensure. In a unique partnership, Educational Testing Service and ISLLC have developed comprehensive performance-based examinations for licensure — the School Leaders Licensure Assessment (SLLA) for principals and the School Superintendents Assessment (SSA) for superintendents. Appendix B and Appendix C give direct evidence for the linkage between the professional practice of the school administrator or the school superintendent and the ISLLC Standards.

Conclusion

In this brief chapter, we have provided some background material on what the ISLLC Standards are, the foundations that support them, and the ways that they are being used to strengthen the leadership profession. The framework that is described in this volume is another chapter in the story of the partnership between ETS, ISLLC, and some of the Consortium's most respected members — NAESP and NASSP. The framework provides all of us in educational leadership with a powerful platform for continuing the work of reculturing the profession across an array of fronts. Because it can be linked to so many of the major leverage points for reform (e.g., professional development and principal evaluation), it promises to occupy a central position in the fight to reshape the profession around learner-centered leadership.

THE EVOLUTION OF LEADERSHIP

Our nation's schools now have at their disposal the national set of ISLLC Standards for School Leaders, described in Chapter 2, that can be used to bring about significant and positive change to schools and improve the chance of success for all our students. These ISLLC Standards for School Leaders can be used to define the practice of school leaders and to engage them and the school community in restructuring the concept of school leadership and refocusing the leader's attention on the primary issues of teaching and learning. As Eddy Van Meter and Cynthia McMinn (2001) observed:

> The Standards provide a "road map" for practicing principals, a blueprint for making a difference in fundamental areas such as fostering teacher professional growth, engaging sustained parental and community involvement, and accomplishing successful student learning (p. 33).

The purpose of *A Framework for School Leaders: Linking the ISLLC Standards to Practice* is to describe a way to relate these Standards to practice and to actually travel using this "road map." To do this it is necessary to create a common language for talking about school leadership and to begin a process of describing various levels of performance that school leaders demonstrate as they attend to the business of school leadership.

As Murphy and Shipman stated earlier in Chapter 2, the ISSLC Standards have begun to change our view of school leadership and they possess the potential for bringing about significant change in leadership. To provide a context for this transformation, we will begin by describing the present status of school leadership in the United States and the events through history that created this current view. Once a clear understanding of the current status is defined, we will show how the Standards can be used to refocus public and professional attitudes about the position of school leaders and describe the link between effective school leadership and productive schools.

As changes have taken place in our society, so have changes taken place in the principalship. This history reflects a continuing evolution of the principalship from an early position of attendance clerk to the present position of a teaching and learning visionary in a standards-based setting. The pace of change has rapidly increased and, in order to survive this complex, dynamic transformation, school leaders need to be adaptable, flexible, and able to learn from the changes.

The principalship has been influenced and shaped by a variety of historical forces. The history of school leadership is clearly a history of the interaction of broad social and intellectual movements within American society. School leadership has undergone significant transformation in an attempt to gain legitimacy within schools (Glanz, 1998).

The first principals were appointed in Cincinnati (1839), Boston (1842), St. Louis (1859), Chicago (1862), and New York (1867). These "principal teachers" were responsible for attendance and enrollment figures and school cleanliness and repairs. The duties were essentially clerical and some released time was provided. The main focus of their work was on management.

In the late 1870's and 1880's, the role of the principal was changed to be the "teacher of teachers." The main focus was on instructing and mentoring poorly prepared teachers in the art of teaching. The concern for the individuality of the teacher was paramount (Bulton, p.22) and the method of supervision was democratic. Additional responsibilities dealt with the traditional tasks of management, i.e., attendance-taking, managing teachers and resources, responding to routine problems, and overseeing the building.

In contrast, the period of 1885 – 1905, influenced by the autocrats, brought about more authoritarian, supervisory methods to focus on dealing with weak and ineffective teachers. Characteristic of the supervisory strategies employed by "autocrats" were the views and practices of William Torrey Harris (1871), who maintained that the "first prerequisite of the school is order" (p. 31). These autocratic practices in supervision were influenced by the centralization of education in the latter part of the century (Calkins, p.2). The needs and demands of the organization became the focus.

The tension between the individual's needs and the organization's needs grew between 1905 and 1920 during the Era of Economy and Efficiency. Supervisory practice was patterned after "...the administrator of business and industrial management view of school organization." Influenced by Taylor, as well as Cubberley and Bobbitt, business and management practices dominated theory and practice. Elaborate rating scales to measure teacher efficiency were used and the scientific approach to supervision emerged (Glanz, p. 41).

Glanz contends that two related, but sometimes opposing processes — bureaucracy and professionalism — shaped supervision between 1875 and 1937. As the number of principals increased and the number and size of the school systems grew in size and complexity, so too did the problems and tensions confronting the supervisor. Due to increasing bureaucratization of urban schools and rating procedures used, other educators sharply criticized the administrators of the early decades of the 20th century. Torn between administrative duties and instructional responsibilities, the supervisor realized his/her precarious status in the bureaucratic hierarchy. "It was in response to mounting criticism that supervisors, in a concerted effort to gain control of their work, sought to professionalize as a means to counteract bureaucracy" (Glanz, p.42).

The dilemma between meeting the demands of the school organization (the bureaucracy) and the drive for professional autonomy (professionalism) was the basis of a struggle between administrative duties and instructional responsibilities. The routines and the industrial, colder view of education then gave way to another phase in education. These struggles lead to an Era of Human Relations where the affective needs of the individual were again in focus.

The era from the 1950's through the close of the 1970's presented the school principal with some of the most significant challenges ever. Our country faced the escalation of both "cold" and "hot" wars that resulted in public discontent spilling over into our universities and schools. Our nation was challenged by the apparent superiority of the Russian school system, manifested by its advanced space technology; engaged in an unpopular war being fought in Southeast Asia; and facing civil unrest here at home. These events resulted in public opinion that was inflamed by the demand for social justice and equity for all. New Supreme Court decisions and their ensuing federal regulations demanded, for the first time, equal educational opportunities for all. Public demands for improved learning, especially in science and mathematics, the inclusion of educationally handicapped students, and the emotions involved in creating integrated schools brought unique challenges for our schools and their leaders.

Beginning in the 1980's, the Age of Reform in school administration is synonymous with the reform of the principalship. The principal must be financial manager, skillful negotiator, manager of human resources, source of legal knowledge, and human relations expert. The challenge of educational leadership in a changing world recognized the broad and deep cultural changes that shaped the study and practice of educational administration.

Throughout much of this history, the focus on leadership was managerial and administrative. The main responsibility of the principalship was maintaining the building, controlling student and staff behavior, and other assorted tasks.

> Being an effective building manager used to be good enough. For the past century, principals were mostly expected to comply with district level edicts, assess personnel issues, order supplies, balance program budgets, keep hallways and playgrounds safe, put out fires that threatened tranquil public relations, and make sure that the busing and meal services were operating smoothly (IEL, 2000, p. 2).

All of these are important in their own way but clearly are not focused on the mission of the educational enterprise: student learning. Richard Elmore (2000) states that, even today,

> ... principals who develop the skills and knowledge required to actually do instructional leadership in a serious way do so because of their personal preferences and values, often at some personal cost to their own careers, not because they are expected to do so as a condition of their work...The institutional structure does not promote, or select for, knowledge and skill related to instructional leadership; at best, it tolerates some proportion of the population who indulge in it out of personal commitment and taste (p. 7).

To meet the needs of our changing society, a new type of leadership is required in the schools. During recent history there has been an effort to redefine learning and teaching in ways to more successfully challenge and engage *all* students in the educational process. A movement to create more community-focused, caring-centered schools and move away from the established notions of schools as bureaucracies is underway. Stakeholders, external to the school building—parents, business leaders, and community leaders —are playing more significant roles in education (Council of Chief State School Officers, p.6).

Upon examining the evolution of school leadership, the focus has always been on the teacher and how the school administrator interacts with him or her. The paradigm shift to a more student-centered view of leadership and the development of clear standards for school leaders occurred in the 1990's with the standards movement, restructuring, and student-centered reform.

This brief history of school leadership can be summarized in Figure 3.1 on the following page.

An Overview of the History of School Leadership: Interaction of Social and Intellectual Movements in American Society

SCHOOL LEADERSHIP	ROLE
1839 – 1867: First "Principal Teachers" appointed	▓ Clerical ▓ Attendance ▓ School repair
1870 – 1880: Principal as "teacher of teachers"	▓ Instructing and mentoring teachers in the art of teaching
1885 – 1905: Era of Authoritarian Supervision	▓ Dealing with weak and ineffective teachers ▓ Centralization of education ▓ Organizational, orderly focus
1905 – 1920: Era of Efficiency and Economy	▓ Scientific Management ▓ Business and industrial management view of school organization ▓ Elaborate rating scales to measure teacher efficiency used
1920 – 1938: Improvement of Instruction	▓ School leader becomes more democratic and professional ▓ Management is still a focus
1938 – 1950: Era of Human Relations	▓ Expansion of democratic methods — cooperation with and consideration of teacher
1950 – 1980: Era of Professionalism	▓ Professionalism of school leaders and curriculum workers ▓ Cold and Hot Wars ▓ Impact of Supreme Court Rulings (education opportunities for all) ▓ Science and Math focus ▓ Inclusion of handicapped ▓ Integration

1980: Age of Reform	▓ Principal serves as:
	  – Financial manager
	  – Negotiator
	  – Manager of human resources
	  – Source of legal knowledge
	  – Human relations expert

1990 to present	▓ Standards movement ▓ Restructuring ▓ Student-centered reform

The Standards Movement

Until recently, the standards movement focused its attention on the student and teacher. Logically, this made the most sense because the primary mission of the school leader is to ensure student learning within the school, brought about by effective teaching. In *Leading School Improvement: What Research Says*, Hoachlander, Alt, and Beltranena (2001) state that the most direct method of raising academic and technical content of courses is explicit attention to standards, in both the curriculum and assessments. Efforts at the state and national levels have tried to define clearly what students will know and be expected to do to prepare them for work (p.15).

Indeed, no reform initiative has translated into as much academic success for students and provided such a clear focus for teachers as has the standards movement.

> Content standards for student learning articulate the entire domain of learning in a particular area. Well-written standards emphasize understanding of a discipline's foundations of knowledge, not discrete bits of knowledge and mastery of particular techniques. And if student standards define achievement as the demonstration of understanding, the implications for instruction are profound. Equally profound are the implications for the professional development of both teachers and principals (Holloway and Pearlman, 2001, p. 40).

There is, by now, general agreement between educators and community leaders that higher standards are a core component of the reform process and these standards are necessary to assure the success of our students and the very survival of the public schools. The standards movement, exemplified by descriptions and definitions of excellence in teaching, as in Danielson's *Enhancing Professional Practice: A Framework for Teaching*, and by descriptions of excellence in student performance standards, as in student content and performance standards, has produced powerful side effects. It has long been recognized that articulating clear standards for student learning, illustrated by examples of exemplary student work, enhances the quality of that work and a student's sense of purpose. Teachers have discovered that when they are clear to students about criteria to evaluate a project or paper, students are far more focused and the resultant project or paper is of higher quality than when the criteria are not clear. Students who desire to self assess as a means of improving their work can clearly refer to the rubric and know exactly what is expected. The same phenomenon, identification of high standards with the attendant powerful consequences for practice, is at work in the framework for teaching, which offers a structure to assess a teacher's practice and to organize improvement efforts.

Reframed Purposes of Education

The standards-based reforms, along with the reframed purposes of schooling, form the basis of schooling today (Zemelman, Daniels, Hyde, 1998, p.4). Those reframed purposes posit that problem solving, along with solid understanding of a core body of knowledge and core values, lie at the heart of the new citizen. It is critical for our school leaders to be able to identify and internalize those aspects of administrative responsibility that promote student achievement and success.

Student-centered Reform

At the very core of the school leader's role is a focus on improved classroom instruction to ensure student learning and success for all.

> The bottom line of schooling, after all, is student learning. Everything principals do — establishing a vision, setting goals, managing staff, rallying the community, creating effective learning environments, building support systems for students, guiding instruction, and so on — must be in service of student learning. (IEL, 2000, p.4).

These efforts require an empowered faculty, staff, and student body. The hallmarks of an effective school, with an effective leader, are all related to students and their success. The very mission of an effective school is improved academic achievement and success of all students in the community, leading to effective responsible citizenship. Students, in a school with an effective leader, are held in high regard. There is respect given to their families, to whom the school belongs. Teachers and administrators feel privileged to work together for student success. A strong focus on best practices in teaching and learning, tied directly to student success, is employed in this school. Strong staff development programs, held to high expectations, are aligned to the data-driven needs of the students.

Standards for School Leadership

The imperative to improving schooling for all students, then, is marked by a strong standards movement for teaching and learning, by reframed purposes, and by a clear and insistent focus on student achievement for all students. To ensure that these reforms are truly effective, school leaders must also be guided by, and model their practice on, a set of standards that embraces and supports the new student and teacher standards, the new purposes, and the new imperative for success for all students.

Research affirms that effective principal leadership positively affects student achievement and that successful schools are characterized by a clear sense of purpose supported by the instructional leadership of the principal. Effective school leadership, clearly, is essential. According to Robert Evans (1999), "There is no school change effort that I'm aware of that has survived the indifference of the school principal. None." (Evan's videotape). Furthermore, if we are to improve the quality of the schools of America, then the standards encompassing the requisite knowledge, skills, and dispositions of the principal must be clearly defined.

The framework for school administrators described in this book identifies those aspects of an administrator's responsibilities that have been endorsed by many professional organizations. These organizations include the National Policy Board for Educational Administration (NPBEA); the National Council for the Accreditation for Teacher Education (NCATE); and the Chief Council of State School Officers (CCSSO) in its document, *The Interstate School Leaders Licensure Consortium Standards For School Leaders*. The adoption of the ISLLC Standards for School Leaders by the Council of Chief State School Officers, (1996) and the subsequent dissemination of those Standards established a dynamic new portrait of effective school leaders.

As stated by Shipman and Murphy in Chapter 2 of this book, the Standards have had a significant influence on education. NCATE has now adopted the Standards and in Appendix D we show a clear link between the ISLLC Standards and the Technology Standards for School Administrators. This framework seeks to build on these Standards by further defining what school leaders should know and be able to do in their practice and by showing how we might use this structure to describe levels of performance. The overall purpose, then, is to build on the strong foundation of the ISLLC Standards in a way that will positively impact the development and recognition of effective school leaders.

THE EFFECTIVE SCHOOL LEADER AND THE ISLLC STANDARDS

Effective school leaders make a difference: a difference between failure and success, a difference between inertia and progress, a difference between sufficiency and excellence. The school leader shapes an environment that promotes the success of all students. This environment energizes and celebrates progress toward achieving challenging goals. Within this environment, the school leader envisions, stimulates, facilitates, and monitors processes and activities designed to fuel excellence within the educational system. The school leader focuses these processes and activities on central issues of learning, teaching, and school improvement. The school leader ensures these processes and activities are explicitly designed to be inclusive of all stakeholders who receive information about the processes and activities, and that their outcomes are promulgated to all. The school leader holds students to be the guiding force behind his or her work. Promoting the success of all students is the powerful lens through which all leadership endeavors are viewed. The school leader bases these endeavors on a belief in the inherent worth and dignity of all. It is the school leader's mission to create a culture that honors and supports that worth and dignity.

The ISLLC Standards presented in Chapter 2 offer an integrated view of what defines an exemplary school leader. The Standards are comprehensive, clearly focused on the school leader as one whose mission is to promote the success of all students.

Knowledge, Disposition, and Performance Indicators

Knowledge, disposition, and performance indicators or statements that mark the work of an effective leader define each of the six Standards. The **knowledge indicators** present the kinds of theories, trends, principles, models, and concepts that serve as a part of the foundation for what the school leader should know and understand. Similarly, the **disposition indicators** present statements of what the school leader should value or believe in. The **performance indicators** describe what the school leader actually does. For example, for Standard 1, the following illustrate just one of the many indicators for each of the knowledge, dispositions, and performance statements:

Knowledge: The administrator has knowledge and understanding of learning goals in a pluralistic society.

Dispositions: The administrator believes in, values, and is committed to the educability of all.

Performances: The administrator facilitates processes and engages in activities ensuring that the vision and mission of the school are effectively communicated to staff, parents, students, and community members.

The complete Standards and each of their accompanying knowledge, dispositions, and performance indicators can be viewed online at www.ccsso.org.

Central Themes

A consideration of all six Standards, taken as a whole, suggests that there are broad **themes** that run across the Standards. Educational Testing Service has discovered some of these central **themes** by engaging school leaders and content experts from around the United States in many formal reviews of the Standards. Based upon these reviews, four recurring central **themes** emerged. These unifying themes create a redefined vision of effective school leadership and reflect the school leader's primary responsibility of promoting the success of all students. The themes inform all aspects of a coordinated effort to enhance and reexamine the roles of school leaders. In addition to their use in this framework for school leaders, the themes and the Standards from which they are drawn provide the foundation for new systems of school leader licensure assessment, portfolios used for assessment or professional growth, and other programs for professional development. A careful analysis of the Standards will uncover many themes or threads that unify them and their associated indicators. However, these four central recurring **themes** seem most evident:

- A Vision for Success

- A Focus on Teaching and Learning

- An Involvement of all Stakeholders

- A Demonstration of Ethical Behavior

A Vision for Success

Effective leaders employ recursive systems for envisioning, planning, implementing, and evaluating processes, programs, and activities.

The effective school leader works for continuous school improvement achieved through a cyclical, or recursive, process in which the school's vision, mission, and strategic plans are developed, implemented, monitored, evaluated, and revised. The leader understands the change process, and knows that part of that process is the systematic examination of assumptions, beliefs, and practices and of the school culture and climate. The process includes also identifying, clarifying, and addressing barriers to achieving the school's vision. The effective leader assures that the process is inclusive, involving all stakeholders.

The leader knows and acts upon appropriate theories and models of organization. He or she uses a variety of information sources, including assessment and demographic data, to make decisions The leader assures that issues, trends, and political, social, cultural, and economic systems and processes that impact schools are applied in the change process. The leader also assures that this process incorporates research, expectations of teachers, and recommendations of professional organizations. The effective leader assures that through this change process, appropriate curricular, co-curricular, and extra-curricular programs are designed, implemented, evaluated, and refined. Requisite resources for implementation are sought and, whenever possible, obtained.

He or she understands and supports the role of public education in developing and renewing a democratic society and an economically productive nation. The effective leader knows that his or her influence and responsibility extend beyond the school; he or she actively participates in arenas of political and public policy-making in the service of education.

A Focus on Teaching and Learning

Teaching and learning lie at the heart of the school leader's mission.

Central to this theme is the focus on teaching and learning as opposed to primarily managerial duties. The unwavering commitment to high standards for all, to a culture of high expectations, and to a belief that all students can learn is clearly identified throughout the ISLLC Standards. To meet this commitment, the school leader assures that barriers to student learning are identified, clarified, and addressed and that all appropriate stakeholders are involved in the education and decision-making process.

The centrality of teaching and learning mandates that the effective school leader have knowledge of human growth and development, and of theories of motivation. Effective teaching and learning programs require pupil personnel programs that meet the needs of students and parents, and an integration of school and community programs for youth and family services.

The commitment to teaching and learning requires knowledge of curriculum design, implementation, evaluation, and refinement; of effective instruction including knowledge of appropriate use of teaching strategies and materials including technology; and of appropriate and effective measurement, evaluation, and assessment strategies. Activities and programs to enhance teaching and learning are based on diversity; the effective leader must have a knowledge of a variety of approaches, responsive to varied student needs, that assure that students have multiple opportunities to learn and demonstrate learning.

The leader must have knowledge of the importance of effective school cultures, assuring safe and supportive learning environments. To support effective learning and teaching programs within these environments, the school leader must have knowledge of and belief in effective professional development focused on student learning.

As conceived of in the ISLLC Standards, knowledge of learning, teaching, and student development is used to inform management decisions that provide a safe, efficient, and effective learning environment. Priorities for learning and teaching programs designed to promote success for all students govern issues of operational procedures, organization, and resources including human resources, public resources and funds, facilities, space, and time. The effective school leader confronts and resolves potential problems involving management issues to assure effective learning and teaching will be impacted as positively as possible.

The centrality of teaching and learning to maximize success for all students is essential in every aspect of the school leader's responsibilities.

An Involvement of all Stakeholders

Inclusive, representative governance built on a belief in the worth
and dignity of all is essential for effective leadership.

The effective school leader bases all processes and activities on principles of representative governance that undergird American schools. Such a leader is committed to and skilled in consensus building, collaboration, and group processes, and shares responsibilities to maximize ownership and accountability. These principles of governance guide the leader's actions in problem framing and problem solving, conflict resolution, and negotiation.

The effective leader involves all stakeholders in school governance whenever possible including in the development of a vision, in school improvement efforts, and in management processes. The leader knows and employs successful partnership models involving school, family, business, community, government, and higher education. The leader knows the importance of collaboration with and outreach to families and community, and to business, religious, political, and service agencies and organizations.

In schools governed by effective leaders, all individuals are treated with fairness, equity, dignity, and respect; all stakeholders feel valued and important. The responsibilities and contributions of each individual are recognized and celebrated. The effective school leader trusts people and their judgments; and gives credence to individuals and groups whose values and opinions may conflict.

Inclusive, representative governance relies on a comprehensive communication system. The leader models the core beliefs of the school's vision and disseminates progress toward the vision and mission to all. Contributions of school community members to the realization of the vision are recognized and celebrated. The effective school leader demonstrates the importance of an informed public, and employs a comprehensive program of community relations. This program involves high visibility, active involvement, and communication with the larger community. The effective leader engages in ongoing dialogue with other decision-makers and representatives of diverse community groups.

A Demonstration of Ethical Behavior

Effective leaders have a strong commitment to ethical behavior and are moral agents and social advocates for students, families, and communities.

An effective school leader demonstrates both respect for a pluralistic society and a commitment to students as individuals. The leader holds a firm belief that all students can learn, and holds and insists on high standards, expectations, and performances.

Such a leader values, appreciates, and is sensitive to diversity in the school community. The leader examines and considers the prevailing values, conditions, and dynamics of the diverse school community, and the significance of diversity for educational programs.

Everything an effective school leader does is governed by a personal and professional code of ethics. Decisions are rooted in the ideal of the common good and the principles of the *Bill of Rights*. The leader works to sustain and improve humane conditions for all. The leader subordinates personal interests to the good of the school community. The leader uses the influence of the office constructively in the service of all students and their families.

The leader trusts people and their judgments, and takes appropriate risks to improve schools. The leader defends the rights of all students, families, and staff, including the right to confidentiality and privacy. The school leader meets fully all legal and contractual obligations; and applies laws and procedures fairly, wisely, and considerately.

THE FRAMEWORK: AN OVERVIEW
Purposes

While the *ISLLC Standards for School Leaders* define the elements of appropriate practice, they are not meant to measure, assess or analyze behaviors of leaders or the various ways school leaders articulate or implement these Standards. The overarching purpose of the framework presented in this book is to bridge this gap by linking the Standards to the practice of the school leader. Three specific goals define the structure, the organization, and the content of this framework:

⊕ To serve as a foundation and to provide a common language for redefining and refocusing the role of the school leader as defined by the ISLLC Standards

⊕ To articulate the role of the school leader as defined by the ISLLC Standards

⊕ To serve as a standards-based approach to describe various school leaders' levels of performance

The ISLLC Standards themselves are envisioned as presenting "a common core of knowledge, dispositions, and performances that will help link leadership more forcefully to productive schools and enhanced educational outcomes" (Council of Chief State School Officers, 1996. Introduction). This common core provides the foundation for effective leadership; the discussions of the Standards themselves provide the common language for the redefinition and refocusing of the role of the school leader.

To translate theory into practice, the framework presents each of the six Standards as a set of four Components of Professional Practice for School Leaders, or specific aspects of the Standards. These 24 components summarize all the indicators that define the Standards and serve to articulate the role of the school leader, as they highlight and discuss features of the Standards that are essential to the school leader's enhanced role. The components are designed to make all the information contained within the Standards and their indicators more manageable by distilling the essential features of each Standard into four concise phrases. The Components of Professional Practice for School Leaders follow:

Components of Professional Practice for School Leaders

STANDARD 1: THE VISION OF LEARNING
- 1a. Developing the Vision
- 1b. Communicating the Vision
- 1c. Implementing the Vision
- 1d. Monitoring and Evaluating the Vision

STANDARD 2: THE CULTURE OF TEACHING AND LEARNING
- 2a. Valuing Students and Staff
- 2b. Developing and Sustaining the Culture
- 2c. Ensuring an Inclusive Culture
- 2d. Monitoring and Evaluating the Culture

STANDARD 3: THE MANAGEMENT OF LEARNING
- 3a. Making Management Decisions to Ensure Successful Teaching and Learning
- 3b. Developing Procedures to Ensure Successful Teaching and Learning
- 3c. Allocating Resources to Ensure Successful Teaching and Learning
- 3d. Creating a Safe, Healthy Environment to Ensure Successful Teaching and Learning

STANDARD 4: RELATIONSHIPS WITH THE BROADER COMMUNITY TO FOSTER LEARNING
- 4a. Understanding Community Needs
- 4b. Involving Members of the Community
- 4c. Providing Opportunities for the Community and School to Serve Each Other
- 4d. Understanding and Valuing Diversity

STANDARD 5: INTEGRITY, FAIRNESS, AND ETHICS IN LEARNING
- 5a. Demonstrating a Personal and Professional Code of Ethics
- 5b. Understanding One's Impact on the School and Community
- 5c. Respecting the Rights and Dignity of All
- 5d. Inspiring Integrity and Ethical Behavior in Others

STANDARD 6: THE POLITICAL, SOCIAL, ECONOMIC, LEGAL, AND CULTURAL CONTEXT OF LEARNING
- 6a. Operating Schools on Behalf of Students and Families
- 6b. Communicating Changes in Environment to Stakeholders
- 6c. Working Within Policies, Laws, and Regulations
- 6d. Communicating with Decision-Makers Outside the School Community

These components form the foundation of 24 **Component Performance Tables.** These tables summarize descriptors of four performance levels for each of the 24 components by capturing school leader behaviors within each of the four central themes, described on pages 21 – 25, that weave through the ISLLC Standards. These tables, collectively, become the framework for school leaders and provide a vehicle for quickly describing school leader behavior. The framework serves a variety of purposes that range from use as a powerful guide for preparing aspiring, novice school leaders to use by the experienced, veteran leader as an aid in reflecting on his or her current professional practice. Most importantly, the framework, as defined by its related performance tables, provides a common language for describing the behaviors of school leaders and their performances. They thus provide the educational community with a shared understanding of the performance of school leaders and as a basis for a shared pursuit of excellence.

Each of the Component Performance Tables defines four levels of performance. These levels are:

- Rudimentary
- Developing
- Proficient
- Accomplished

Upon reviewing these four levels of performance and then reflecting on their application to the following 24 Component Performance Tables, two issues become quite clear. First, no one individual will perform at the same level in each component. Many different levels will characterize an individual's performance across all the components, and this is to be expected. What one would expect is a bumpy ride across the components with peaks and valleys and few, if any, level patches of road. Second, the descriptors within the tables are designed to be applicable to many different school leader positions (e.g., principal, superintendent, etc.) and suitable to various school types, locations, and settings. This design gives users the opportunity to attach a variety of meanings and context to the individual table cells. As such, each Standard description is framed by areas of focus defined by knowledge and skills, which may be evidenced at different levels of performance on the rubric tables. These tables are a guide or template and it is incumbent on the reader to take this into consideration and find specific examples within each table cell that will suit his or her circumstances. Finally, the presentation of the Component Performance Tables was intentionally chosen to reflect the architecture of the rubrics used in scoring the assessments found in the ISLLC School Leadership Series of licensure assessment. The same language is inherent in the tables and in the scoring rubrics. Furthermore, each table is specifically designed to "stand alone." Thus, there are no references to other tables or rubrics in any of the framework tables and this, sometimes out of necessity, leads to some repetition in the wording from table to table.

The structure of a typical table (Component 1d) for one of the central themes (A Vision for Success) is illustrated as follows:

The **RUDIMENTARY** level typically describes that "little or no evidence" exists for the set of behaviors called for by the specific component. It is important to note that the designation of "rudimentary" does not necessarily mean that the school leader is not capable overall or not capable of the specific set of behaviors found within the component. Instead, this designation simply means that there is little or no evidence of achievement of the component judged by performance.

The **DEVELOPING** level typically describes "limited" evidence. The evidence may not address the component in its complexity, may be lacking in breadth or depth, or may be less effective than is expected. For example, the school leader may be aware of the fact that stakeholders should be involved in the decision-making process, but there is only limited evidence that the leader knows when or how to get them involved, or is consistent with this fundamental practice over time.

LEVEL OF PERFORMANCE				
Central Themes*	**Rudimentary**	**Developing**	**Proficient**	**Accomplished**
A Vision for Success	There is little or no evidence that the school leader either collects or analyzes data about the school's progress toward realizing the vision.	There is limited evidence that the school leader collects data on the school's progress toward the vision or uses this information to promote student success in any meaningful way.	There is clear evidence that the school leader collects data periodically on the school's progress toward the vision and uses this information to make decisions that promote the success of students.	There is clear, convincing, and consistent evidence that the school leader collects and analyzes data on the school's progress toward realizing the vision throughout the school year and continually uses this information to make decisions that promote the success of all students.

The level of **PROFICIENT** typically describes "clear" evidence. The evidence is specific and reasonable, and addresses the complexity of the component. At times, the evidence may be somewhat uneven, with specific features within the component addressed more effectively than others. In general, the evidence shows that the school leader knows what to do and does it.

The level of **ACCOMPLISHED** typically describes "clear, convincing, and consistent" evidence. The evidence is very specific and credible. It is comprehensive and thoughtful, presenting an integrated, highly effective approach to the behaviors specified in the component.

THE FRAMEWORK FOR SCHOOL LEADERS

This chapter describes the framework for school leaders and its related six ISLLC Standards, the 24 components, and the 24 Component Performance Tables. Each Standard is restated and is briefly described. Following that introductory information, the Standard's four related components are defined and the performance table for each is presented. These tables are organized around two key concepts: the central themes and the levels of performance, both defined and described in Chapters 4 and 5. The central themes create a redefined vision of effective school leadership and reflect the school leader's primary responsibility of promoting the success of all students. The themes inform all aspects of a coordinated effort to enhance and reexamine the role of school leaders.

The four central recurring themes are:

- A Vision for Success

- A Focus on Teaching and Learning

- An Involvement of all Stakeholders

- A Demonstration of Ethical Behavior

The four performance levels are:

- Rudimentary

- Developing

- Proficient

- Accomplished

A school administrator is an educational leader who promotes the success of all students by facilitating the development, articulation, implementation, and stewardship of a school or district vision of learning that is shared and supported by the school community (CCSSO, 1996, p. 10).

STANDARD **1**

The purpose of this Standard is to ensure that school administrators have a keen sense of their responsibility for developing and articulating a vision of learning for their school community. School administrators must believe in their primary mission of educating all students to acquire the knowledge, skills, and values necessary to become successful adults. It is the responsibility of each administrator to create and articulate this vision of high standards of learning within the school or district so that it is shared and supported by the entire school community, both within the school building and in the broader school community of parents and citizens. To engage the entire school community in this enterprise, administrators must examine their own assumptions, beliefs, and practices, and foster a climate of continuous improvement involving all members of the school community. Such administrators commit themselves to high levels of personal and organizational performance in order to assure that this vision of learning is implemented (National Policy Board of Education Administration).

Each Standard is framed by areas of focus defined by knowledge and skills, which may be evidenced at different levels of performance as indicated on the accompanying rubric tables. These areas of focus may be applied in different ways on the rubric tables. The leadership position (e.g., principal, superintendent, etc.) and context (e.g., elementary, secondary, urban, suburban, etc.) will determine their use.

STANDARD 1: THE VISION OF LEARNING

Areas of Focus	Knowledge and Skills
Facilitation Skills	▥ fosters the development of a vision for learning and the components of this vision to promote the success of all students ▥ articulates the vision for all stakeholders through a variety of communication modes ▥ articulates the processes necessary to achieve the vision ▥ communicates effectively with all stakeholders on the implementation of the vision
Challenging Standards	▥ builds a shared commitment to high standards of learning and achievement for all students
Strategic Planning Process	▥ facilitates development of objectives and strategies in the implementation plan and process to implement the vision effectively ▥ demonstrates how strategic planning processes focus on student learning, inform the vision, and draw on relevant sources of student achievement data and demographic data pertaining to students and their families ▥ monitors, evaluates and revises the plan
Building Leadership Capacity	▥ facilitates collegiality and teamwork ▥ delegates responsibility and develops leadership in others ▥ structures significant work
Community Involvement	▥ involves school community members in realization of the vision and in related school improvement efforts

Developing the Vision

School leaders in New Jersey understand the importance of creating a vision for their schools and how this vision must become the focus of their decision-making processes. Embedded in our professional development offerings, school leaders are frequently asked to reflect on how any decision that they might make will advance the vision of their school and how this decision will contribute to the success of all students. Through our work with principals from virtually every school in our state, we have learned that the vision of the school, developed collaboratively with all members of the school community, provides the school leader with direction, purpose, and a commitment to what we are all about.

JoAnn Bartoletti, Executive Director
New Jersey Principals and Supervisors Association

At the very core of the leader's mission is the development of a vision. This vision shapes all educational programs, plans, and activities. The vision is based on certain essential values and kinds of knowledge that serve as its foundation. Chief among these is the school leader's commitment to the educability of all children and adherence to high expectations for their success. In formulating the school vision, it is essential that the school leader believe in the true inclusion of all members of the school community. It is critical that the school leader has knowledge of the school and its context.

Generally guided by the district's mission statement and strategic plan, a school leader aligns his or her vision and goals with those of the district, based on the identified academic and developmental needs of the student body.

> "... the vision of the school, developed collaboratively with all members of the school community, provides the school leader with direction, purpose, and a commitment to what we are all about. "

Collecting appropriate information from a variety of available sources, the school leader analyzes the data and begins to uncover trends that need to be addressed. In the development of the school mission and goals, the school leader also considers relevant demographic data pertaining to the students and their families. The leader assumes that the areas in need of improvement will have appropriate, measurable targets set indicating the increased academic performance or achievement level anticipated.

The leader then assumes that learning goals that speak to the vision and mission of the school are developed with the input of stakeholders, and that all individual teachers, teams, and departments align their goals and individual growth and improvement plans with the school goals. Each program, plan, and activity at the school must be connected and contribute to the overall success of the school vision. "Effective school leaders are strong educators, anchoring their work on central issues of learning and teaching and school improvement" (CCSSO, 1996, p. 5). Student learning and continued growth form the focus of this Standard.

Figure 6.1: Component 1a

STANDARD 1: THE VISION OF LEARNING

A school administrator is an educational leader who promotes the success of all students by facilitating the development, articulation, implementation, and stewardship of a vision for learning that is shared and supported by the community.

Component 1a: Developing the Vision — Component Performance Table

	LEVEL OF PERFORMANCE			
Central Themes *	**Rudimentary**	**Developing**	**Proficient**	**Accomplished**
A Vision for Success	There is little or no evidence that the school leader has created a vision for the school.	There is limited evidence that the school leader has created a vision that will ensure the success of all students, and there is limited evidence that it is integrated into the school program.	There is clear evidence that the school leader has created a vision that attempts to ensure the success of all students, and/or creates one that is applied consistently in most cases throughout the school program.	There is clear, convincing, and consistent evidence that the school leader has created a vision of success that includes all students and that is consistently integrated throughout the school program.
A Focus on Teaching and Learning	There is little or no evidence that the school leader includes any reference to teaching and learning in the vision.	There is limited evidence that the school leader has considered some aspects of teaching and learning in the development of the vision.	There is clear evidence that the school leader uses the vision to shape most educational programs, plans, and actions.	There is clear, convincing, and consistent evidence that the school leader has developed the vision based on a focus on the success of all students and the vision is embedded in all educational programs, plans, activities, and actions.
An Involvement of all Stakeholders	There is little or no evidence that any members of the school community were involved in the creation of the vision.	There is limited evidence that the school leader has involved appropriate stakeholders in developing the vision, and/or that these individuals were involved appropriately.	There is clear evidence that appropriate stakeholders participated in the development of the vision, and/or consistently throughout the process.	There is clear, convincing, and consistent evidence that the school leader has included representatives of all appropriate members of the community in the development of the vision and that they shared in all the decision-making processes.
A Demonstration of Ethical Behavior	There is little or no evidence that the school leader considered the needs of all students in an equitable manner in the development of the school vision.	There is limited evidence that the school leader has used student data from all students in an equitable manner to inform the development of the school vision.	There is clear evidence that the school leader used some data about all students in the development of the vision in an equitable manner.	There is clear, convincing, and consistent evidence that the school leader used a variety of sources of data for all students, obtained both in and outside the school, in the development of a vision that is fair and equitable to all.

*These are the four central themes that unify the six Standards. They are fully described in Chapter 4 of this book.

COMPONENT ONE B

Communicating the Vision

To be an effective school leader you have to have a vision not only for the school but also for yourself. A vision is how we would like something to be. It drives us to achieve our objectives both personally and professionally. I believe that a vision not shared is a vision lost. In working with prospective school leaders I take the time to have them look inside themselves, pull to the surface what they believe and share it with others. We must continually work to share our vision with others. In doing so we bring out the best in our students, our community and ourselves.

Dr. Michael "Mick" Arnold
Southern Baptist University
Bolivar, Missouri

Sergiovanni (1992) has described the role of the school leader in communicating the vision of the school as the "high priest," the one who seeks to define, strengthen, and articulate those enduring values, beliefs, and cultural strands that give the school its identity. The net effect of vision communication is to bond students, staff members, parents, and the community in the work of the school. Accomplished school leaders communicate the vision and mission of the school by demonstrating understanding of and clearly articulating a shared and supported vision for learning to all stakeholders. Communicating the vision is perhaps the most important way for a principal to exert leadership. There should be no doubt about what priorities have been established for the school. The principal through words and deeds models the goals and behaviors in such a way that all stakeholders know what is valued. The leader is aware of the value of these actions and how they influence the school culture. Frequent reference is made to the goals. Staff development meetings, parent meetings, faculty meetings, student assemblies, and community informational meetings all focus on these priorities. At any time, anywhere, anyone is able to articulate precisely why they are doing what they are doing and how it is related to the school's goals and mission.

The "how" of communicating the vision is as important as the "what." A keyword here is honesty. All stakeholders need and deserve full, detailed, and accurate information about every aspect of the vision. Perhaps the two most important steps requiring honest communication are at the beginning and at the end: giving stakeholders full and timely information so they can be involved, and providing them full and honest information about how the vision is being realized — both the successes and the disappointments. The accomplished school leader also invites a public dialogue about the vision to provide information to assist in bringing about positive change. Effective communication depends on the skillful use of a wide variety of appropriate media. The school leader is an effective writer and speaker and draws upon the talents of others skilled in these areas. Communication must be appropriate to the audience; the language, tone, and format specially designed to meet their needs. Communication is personal, using the culture of the school to bring meaning of the vision to life. Ultimately perhaps the most effective communication of the vision of the school is through the leader's actions that embody the vision.

> *"... a vision not shared is a vision lost. "*

Communication does not come solely out of the principal's office. The school goals are communicated in a variety of ways. As a result of aligned goals, clear communication is embraced and established by all (i.e., the counselors, the teachers, teams, departments, parent groups, community members). These goals are referenced in such documents as newsletters, bulletins, and budget allocations.

The importance of the voice of the students and parents is communicated through their involvement. The value of the staff's opinions is reflected in the solicitation of their input regularly on all major issues.

Data about the school's performance is provided to the teachers, parents, staff, and community on an ongoing basis. After review and analysis, the progress toward the vision and mission is communicated to all stakeholders.

Additionally the vision and mission are communicated through the use of symbols, ceremonies, stories, and other activities. Through these logos, themes and reminders, the leader makes it known that everyone in the school has a common mission.

STANDARD 1: THE VISION OF LEARNING

A school administrator is an educational leader who promotes the success of all students by facilitating the development, articulation, implementation, and stewardship of a vision for learning that is shared and supported by the community.

Component 1b: Communicating the Vision — Component Performance Table

	LEVEL OF PERFORMANCE			
Central Themes *	**Rudimentary**	**Developing**	**Proficient**	**Accomplished**
A Vision for Success	There is little or no evidence that the school leader communicates the vision to the school community.	There is limited evidence that the school leader communicates the vision appropriately; evidence may be of limited scope or depth.	There is clear evidence that the school leader periodically communicates the vision to the school community.	There is clear, convincing, and consistent evidence that the vision is effectively communicated by the school leader throughout the school year and in a variety of ways, and that the communication supports the success of all students.
A Focus on Teaching and Learning	There is little or no evidence that the communication of the vision by the school leader focuses on issues of teaching and learning.	There is limited evidence that the communication of the vision by the school leader focuses on teaching or learning, but not both, and does not link them in any meaningful way.	There is clear evidence that the communication of the vision by the school leader reveals a clear link between teaching and learning.	There is clear, convincing, and consistent evidence that communication of the vision by the school leader clearly focuses on teaching and its impact on learning and student success, and that this recognition occurs throughout the year and in a variety of venues, both in the school and in the community.
An Involvement of all Stakeholders	There is little or no evidence that the school leader has communicated the vision to stakeholders or that stakeholders have an opportunity to communicate that vision among themselves.	There is limited evidence to show that stakeholders are aware of the vision and were engaged in discussion of the vision.	There is clear evidence that the school leader provides a forum for stakeholders to annually engage in a dialogue about the vision.	There is clear, convincing, and consistent evidence that the school leader has provided an opportunity for all stakeholders to engage in a discussion about the vision throughout the school year, both in and out of the school.
A Demonstration of Ethical Behavior	There is little or no evidence that the school leader has communicated the vision openly, honestly, and sensitively to all stakeholders.	There is limited evidence that the school leader has made an attempt to communicate the vision in a way that is sensitive to the diversity and needs of all stakeholders.	There is clear evidence that the school leader communicates the vision in a way that is sensitive to the needs and diversity of the community, but might not provide for a complete, critical, public debate.	There is clear, convincing, and consistent evidence that the school leader openly, honestly, and sensitively communicates the vision to all stakeholders and provides for a complete, critical, public debate.

*These are the four central themes that unify the six Standards. They are fully described in Chapter 4 of this book

Implementing the Vision

How I wish someone had stressed to me the importance of a school vision when I was a beginning principal. Now, working with aspiring principals, I emphasize the necessity of tying every situation and action to the school vision. It is the principal's responsibility to share and promote the vision so it can be implemented into all facets of the learning community. To do so, I instruct future principals to attend civic and community meetings, utilize the media, invite the public to school, and constantly keep their teachers, students, and staff "vision" focused. This is essential to the principalship.

Patrick A. Bashaw
Educational Administration Department
Harding University
Searcy, Arkansas

The school leader makes powerful instruction the number one, ongoing priority in the school. The school leader is committed to doing the work necessary to reach high levels of personal and organizational performance, continuously using information about student performance to guide improvements. Ensuring that students have the knowledge, skills, and values necessary to become successful adults, the school leader implements a strategic plan. This collaboratively developed plan, in which detailed and specific objectives and strategies are clearly and consistently articulated and supported, transforms the vision into reality. The plan is written in straightforward language accessible to all stakeholders.

The leader assures that there is an alignment of resources and efforts to achieve the school vision, and that patterns in the data are identified and interpreted. He or she makes sure an analysis of the barriers to student achievement is completed and strategies and programs to address these needs are designed and implemented. These might take the form of extended learning periods, second chance learning, modifications, and adaptations to instruction.

The implementation plan consists of a series of connected strategies that:

- Identify what needs to be done (determined by the data analysis)

- Define how to accomplish it (including, if necessary, a curriculum response and a staff development response)

- Identify the needed resources (time, budget, professional growth)

- Outline the timeframe and benchmark measures

"It is the principal's responsibility to share and promote the vision so it can be implemented into all facets of the learning community."

The implementation plan connects to the issues and challenges facing the school. The plan addresses instructional, co-curricular, and extra-curricular programs. It is inclusive, addressing both the current needs and future goals and plans for all students. The accomplished administrator is willing to continuously examine his or her own assumptions, beliefs, and practices (ISLLC Standard 1). The implementation plan must be dynamic rather than static; if the need for adjustments to objectives and strategies is identified during implementation, those adjustments are made with the involvement of all who participated in the development of the original plan and with full disclosure. The plan recognizes the diversity of the community and the needs and abilities of all its students, and uses this information to implement the vision in a fair and equitable way. This continuous assessment, reflection on, and revision of instructional activities allows for effectively meeting the needs of all students. The implementation plan provides for a comprehensive program of staff development, providing the knowledge and skills teachers and others need to meet the objectives and use the strategies of the plan.

Monitoring the impact of curriculum on teaching and learning supports appropriate curriculum revisions and staff development opportunities. There is a clear focus on student achievement, which is supported through study groups, observations, and action research. Stakeholders participate in these activities to ensure the goals of the vision and missions are met.

Finally, the school leader seeks and obtains available and needed resources, both human and fiscal, to support the implementation of the plan. The accomplished school leader marshals resources, seeks out additional resources when needed, in an unwavering pursuit of the school's goals related to student learning. The accomplished school leader is successful in securing these necessary resources to support the plan both through the traditional budgetary process and through external sources of revenue.

Figure 6.3: Component 1c

STANDARD 1: THE VISION OF LEARNING

A school administrator is an educational leader who promotes the success of all students by facilitating the development, articulation, implementation, and stewardship of a vision for learning that is shared and supported by the community.

Component 1c: Implementing the Vision — Component Performance Table

	LEVEL OF PERFORMANCE			
Central Themes *	**Rudimentary**	**Developing**	**Proficient**	**Accomplished**
A Vision for Success	There is little or no evidence that the school leader linked the school program, policy, or procedures to the vision of the school.	There is limited evidence that the school leader has linked the school program to the vision of the school, and where that linkage does occur, it is only done superficially.	There is clear evidence that the school leader has embedded the vision throughout most school programs, policies, and procedures.	There is clear, convincing, and consistent evidence that the school leader has thoughtfully aligned and linked all school programs, policies, and procedures to the vision of the school.
A Focus on Teaching and Learning	There is little or no evidence that the school leader has linked any instructional planning, strategies, or student assessment to the vision of the school.	There is limited evidence that the school leader has linked some instructional plans and strategies to the vision of the school and that the school leader interprets or analyzes available data.	There is clear evidence that the school leader has linked most instructional plans and strategies to the vision of the school, and that the school leader uses some student assessment data to inform teaching and learning decisions.	Clear, convincing, and consistent evidence exists that the school leader has embedded the vision in all teaching practices and uses student achievement data to ensure that the vision is firmly focused on the success of all students.
An Involvement of all Stakeholders	There is little or no evidence that the school leader has given members of the school community responsibility for implementing the vision or for allocating resources that support the vision.	There is limited evidence that the school leader has encouraged one or more groups of stakeholders to consider strategies for implementing the vision or for allocating resources that support the vision.	There is clear evidence that the school leader has distributed responsibility for implementing the vision to some members of the school or community and has sought assistance from these individuals in the allocation of resources to support the vision.	There is clear, convincing, and consistent evidence that the school leader has shared responsibility with appropriate stakeholders, in the school and in the community, for implementing the vision and for obtaining and allocating resources to support the vision.
A Demonstration of Ethical Behavior	There is little or no evidence that the school leader has implemented the vision in a way that is sensitive to the diversity within the community or that the vision is focused on the success of all students in a fair and equitable way.	There is limited evidence that the school leader has considered the diversity of the community, or has implemented the vision in a way that addresses the needs of all students and staff in a fair and equitable way.	There is clear evidence that the school leader recognizes the diversity of the community and the needs of the students and staff, and uses some of this information to implement the vision in a fair and equitable way.	There is clear, convincing, and consistent evidence that the school leader recognizes the diversity of the community and the needs and abilities of all students and staff, and uses this information to implement the vision in a way that is fair and equitable to all.

*These are the four central themes that unify the six Standards. They are fully described in Chapter 4 of this book.

Monitoring and Evaluating the Vision

There's no point in developing a vision unless you plan to implement it. If the vision is a big enough stretch to make significant improvements, there will be next steps. All those who must be involved—teachers, staff, parents, students—will need progress reports. A planning group must check frequently and systematically with all the players to see if the steps are in place and working and if they are appropriate. The educational leader must bring people together to talk, think and celebrate progress and they must remain open to adjustments if the plan seems stuck. Without purposeful implementation, the vision could become a mere slogan on the office wall.

Jo Fyfe
Retired Principal and Director of Curriculum
Mt. Diablo Unified School District
Concord, California

As plans to implement the vision are put into action, the school leader must assure that these plans are monitored from the beginning and evaluated over time. The school leader systematically collects and analyzes data on the school progress towards realizing the vision. This monitoring and evaluation must be tied directly to objectives and strategies. Demonstrating a clear understanding of the link between effective teaching and student learning, the school leader also regularly collects data on both student achievement and teacher performance. As appropriate modifications are made in the implementation of the vision, related adjustments must be made to the plan itself.

"The educational leader must bring people together to talk, think and celebrate progress ... "

Monitoring and evaluating the vision, like all aspects of school governance, is an ongoing inclusive process. It includes both informal and formal methods. Stakeholders are afforded opportunities, through such strategies as surveys or questionnaires, open forums, and dialogues, to indicate how well they believe the implementation plan is working. The accomplished school leader invites the appropriate stakeholders to analyze and review this information during the year. Opinions expressed in the public media are carefully considered. Formal monitoring and summative evaluation include use of reliable instruments designed or selected to measure achievement of the goals and effectiveness of the strategies.

Focus throughout the process is upon not only the objectives and strategies, but upon the vision statement itself. A vision is often an idealistic view of what might be, but visions can change with time and circumstance. All stakeholders must be willing to revisit the vision and, in the recursive process of school improvement, ready to create a new vision responsive to change.

STANDARD 1: THE VISION OF LEARNING

A school administrator is an educational leader who promotes the success of all students by facilitating the development, articulation, implementation, and stewardship of a vision for learning that is shared and supported by the community.

Component 1d: Monitoring and Evaluating the Vision — Component Performance Table

	LEVEL OF PERFORMANCE			
Central Themes *	Rudimentary	Developing	Proficient	Accomplished
A Vision for Success	There is little or no evidence that the school leader either collects or analyzes data about the school's progress toward realizing the vision.	There is limited evidence that the school leader collects data on the school's progress toward the vision or uses this information to promote student success in any meaningful way.	There is clear evidence that the school leader collects data periodically on the school's progress toward the vision and uses this information to make decisions that promote the success of students.	There is clear, convincing, and consistent evidence that the school leader collects and analyzes data on the school's progress toward realizing the vision throughout the school year and continually uses this information to make decisions that promote the success of all students.
A Focus on Teaching and Learning	There is little or no evidence that the school leader monitors teacher performance or uses data to assess student learning and progress toward the vision.	There is limited evidence that the school leader monitors either teaching performance or student learning, or that the leader links instruction to student achievement and how this information impacts the school's progress toward realizing the vision.	There is clear evidence that the school leader has created a system to monitor teacher performance and student learning throughout the school year, and demonstrates some understanding of what teaching strategies support increased student learning and progress toward the vision.	There is clear, convincing, and consistent evidence that the school leader collects data on teacher performance and pupil achievement from a variety of sources and demonstrates a clear understanding of how teaching is linked to student learning and what adjustments or modifications must be made to ensure the success of all students and progress toward the vision.
An Involvement of all Stakeholders	There is little or no evidence that the school leader uses data from any stakeholders in assessing progress toward achieving the vision.	There is limited evidence that the school leader gathers information from stakeholders about the school's progress toward the vision, or provides any opportunity for them to analyze or review the data.	There is clear evidence that the school leader collects data about the school's progress toward the vision from a variety of stakeholders and shares this information with the school community. The leader may occasionally provide opportunities for appropriate stakeholders to analyze or review this information.	There is clear, convincing, and consistent evidence that the school leader collects data about progress toward achieving the vision from sources both in and outside the school, and that the leader provides opportunities for appropriate stakeholders to analyze and review this information throughout the school year to ensure that school programs promote the success of all students.
A Demonstration of Ethical Behavior	There is little or no evidence that the school leader uses data on the school's progress toward the vision to report that progress accurately, completely, or frequently.	There is limited evidence that the school leader releases accurate data to the public on the school's progress toward the vision.	There is clear evidence that the school leader provides the community an accurate annual report on the school's progress toward the vision.	There is clear, convincing, and consistent evidence that the school leader uses data on the school's progress toward the vision to provide the school community with accurate, complete, and frequent reports on the status of the vision.

*These are the four central themes that unify the six Standards. They are fully described in Chapter 4 of this bo

A school administrator is an educational leader who promotes the success of all students by advocating, nurturing, and sustaining a school culture and instructional program conducive to student learning and staff professional growth (CCSSO, 1996, p.12).

STANDARD 2

The focus of this Standard is on teaching and learning as the central concerns of the school. It is about accepting the proposition that all students can learn, as well as about the premise that student learning is the fundamental purpose of schools. This Standard requires that administrators be learners who model and encourage life-long learning. To this end, school leaders are responsible for seeing that decisions about curriculum, instructional strategies including the use of instructional technology, assessment, and professional development are based on research literature, professional literature, school and district data, and other contextual information. Success for all students is assured when the school culture and the teaching and learning within the school intersect favorably. All members of the school community have confidence in the integrity of the school improvement decision-making process and the appropriateness of that process for all members of the community. School leaders must demonstrate that all individuals are treated with fairness, dignity, and respect. Successful school administrators identify, clarify, and address barriers to student learning and communicate the importance of teaching and learning for diverse populations. They establish a culture of high expectations for self, student, and staff performance. School leaders are able to assess the culture and climate on a regular basis. They evaluate teacher and staff performance by employing a variety of supervisory models (National Policy Board of Education Administration).

Each Standard is framed by areas of focus defined by knowledge and skills, which may be evidenced at different levels of performance as indicated on the accompanying rubric tables. These areas of focus may be applied in different ways on the rubric tables. The leadership position (e.g., principal, superintendent, etc.) and context (e.g., elementary, secondary, urban, suburban, etc.) will determine their use.

STANDARD 2: THE CULTURE OF TEACHING AND LEARNING

Areas of Focus	Knowledge and Skills
Culture	<ul><li>uses multiple methods to assess and create a school or district culture that recognizes diversity (e.g., language, disability, gender, race, ethnicity, socioeconomic status)</li><li>uses context-appropriate strategies for creating a positive school or district culture</li></ul>
Instructional Program	<ul><li>uses principles of effective instruction, research methods, and other resources</li><li>makes use of and promotes technology and information systems to enrich curriculum and instruction</li><li>develops a school profile, using qualitative and quantitative data, to make recommendations regarding the design, implementation, and evaluation of curriculum that fully accommodate the diverse needs of individual learners</li></ul>
Student Learning	<ul><li>applies human development theories, learning and motivational theories, and concern for diversity to the learning process</li><li>profiles student performance; analyzes possible differences among subgroups of students along relevant characteristics such as race, ethnicity, socioeconomic status, and gender</li><li>promotes an environment for increased student learning and achievement and promotes increased professional competence of staff and self</li></ul>
Professional Growth	<ul><li>designs well-planned and context- appropriate professional development that focuses on student learning, consistent with the school's vision and goals</li><li>develops and implements personal professional growth plans that reflect a commitment to lifelong learning</li></ul>

Valuing Students and Staff

I teach students aspiring to be principals and also those who are practicing administrators who are working toward advanced certification. The students that are aspiring are master's level and those working toward advanced certification are education specialist candidates.

When we talk about culture, the aspiring administrators will concentrate on the climate of the school. They have not yet been in a position to observe the "total school" from a broader perspective. They struggle to think beyond their classrooms. Students at the advanced level are able to think beyond the classroom and look at the impact of the school's culture on the learning environment. This ability is the result of their position and the emphasis placed on the importance of developing and sustaining a learning culture from their earlier exposure to the ISLLC standards. They are able to transfer sound theory into everyday practice.

Dr. John Williams
Central Missouri State University
Warrensburg, Missouri

Successful schools are characterized by a clear sense of purpose supported by the instructional leadership of the principal. All individuals are treated with fairness, dignity, and respect. The school is aligned and organized for success. This foundational purpose is built as a result of a strong culture of shared values, beliefs, and traditions, in which the responsibilities and contributions of each individual are acknowledged. There is a culture of high expectations for self, students, and staff. Celebrating the contributions of staff and students regularly leads to a strong sense of belonging.

You can sense when you are in a school with a powerful collaborative culture as soon as you enter the building. Students and staff feel valued and important. Students, teachers, staff, and administrators are happy and proud to be there. Students talk about the "way we do things around here" and "who we are." They have a voice in the school. Active and responsible dialogue is nurtured and sustained through the voice of all participants in the school, particularly the students. Choice alone cannot build a strong community. Voice is required. Students choose activities that support their communal values. School spirit is ongoing. Student work is on display and the values of the school are evident. These symbols and traditions clearly alert all who enter what is valued, be it academic achievement, community service, respect, random acts of kindness, athletics, attitudes, or hard work. Students begin to model the behavior valued and recognized by their teachers. Students' accomplishments are recognized and celebrated.

Faculty meetings serve as regular forums for teachers to recognize other teachers who have contributed to the overall success of the school in reaching its mission. The teachers begin to model the behavior valued and recognized by the school leader and community. "Culture is a flowing structure. Groups and individuals shape and are shaped by rituals, ceremonies, symbols, icons, rules and relationships." (Saranson, 1971, p.68).

Figure 6.5: Component 2a

STANDARD 2: THE CULTURE OF TEACHING AND LEARNING

A school administrator is an educational leader who promotes the success of all students by advocating, nurturing, and sustaining a school culture and instructional program conducive to student learning and staff professional growth.

Component 2a: Valuing Students and Staff — Component Performance Table

	LEVEL OF PERFORMANCE			
Central Themes *	Rudimentary	Developing	Proficient	Accomplished
A Vision for Success	There is little or no evidence that the school leader recognizes the efforts or accomplishments of students or staff in their support of the school vision.	There is limited evidence that the school leader recognizes the efforts and accomplishments of students or staff in the support of the school vision.	There is clear evidence that the school leader values and recognizes the efforts and accomplishments of students and staff, and reports these periodically during the school year.	There is clear, convincing, and consistent evidence that the school leader values the efforts and accomplishments of all members of the school community and celebrates these successes in a variety of ways, both in and outside the school, throughout the school year.
A Focus on Teaching and Learning	There is little or no evidence that the school leader recognizes the contributions of the teachers or the efforts of the students in the teaching and learning process.	There is limited evidence that the school leader demonstrates appreciation for the contributions of teachers or the achievement of students in the teaching and learning process.	There is clear evidence that the leader values the contributions of the staff and/or the achievements of the students in the teaching and learning process and successes are celebrated on occasion.	There is clear, convincing, and consistent evidence that the school leader understands how the efforts of the staff support the achievement of students and promotes, recognizes, and celebrates these efforts and the achievement of the students in the teaching and learning process throughout the school year.
An Involvement of all Stakeholders	There is little or no evidence to show that the school leader involves the community in recognizing the contributions of teachers or students.	There is limited evidence that the school leader involves stakeholders in the recognition of the success of the teachers and students beyond infrequent routine announcements.	There is clear evidence that the school leader involves all members of the community in celebrating the success of students or teachers, although this recognition may occur only periodically and may be limited to activities held within the school.	There is clear, convincing, and consistent evidence that the school leader involves all members of the community in celebrating the success of students and teachers throughout the school year, and that these celebrations occur within the school and in the community.
A Demonstration of Ethical Behavior	There is little or no evidence to show that the school leader rewards the teaching and learning successes or contributions of students or staff in a fair and equitable way.	There is limited evidence that the school leader rewards the teaching and learning successes of students and teachers in a fair and equitable way.	There is clear evidence that the school leader rewards teaching and learning successes of all groups, although the public recognition may not be uniformly applied over all groups.	There is clear, convincing, and consistent evidence that the school leader treats the teaching and learning contributions and successes of all staff members and students in an equitable and fair way.

*These are the four central themes that unify the six Standards. They are fully described in Chapter 4 of this book.

COMPONENT TWO B

Developing and Sustaining the Culture

It's all about how stakeholders feel! Walking into church on Sunday morning, do you have a feeling? Entering the synagogue on Saturday, is there a feeling? Going to the NCAA finals, is there a feeling? Each day children, teachers, staff members, or parents will have a feeling when they drive up to your school. What's that feeling?

It is the responsibility of the principal to provide the leadership to cultivate a school culture that articulates the vision of the school and community. The job of the principal is to ensure all stakeholders are focused on the highest possible levels of both satisfaction and productivity while providing a safe, orderly, and equal opportunity learning environment. The culture must be so strong that visitors will be able to hear it, see it, smell it, and feel it before they enter the school doors. The culture of teaching and learning should gush out of all the creaks and crevices of every classroom. It's who you are!

Dr. Jack J. Herlihy, Jr.
College of Education
Eastern Kentucky University
Richmond, Kentucky

As Professor Herlihy stated in his introduction to this section, "It is the responsibility of the principal to provide the leadership to cultivate a school culture that articulates the vision of the school and community." That culture is based on the belief that all students can be successful.

In such a culture, flexible delivery of programs is matched with high standards that have been identified for all students. These high standards always remain the target; only the amount of time to "get to" the target varies. There is a culture of high expectations for self, student, and staff performance. A variety of strategies and activities are used in the instructional process. Stakeholders are invited as part of the school community to assist in planning, shaping, and implementing the school programs.

Analysis of the multiple criteria used to evaluate the needs of the students and the teachers leads toward:

- a curriculum tailored to the students' current needs

  Curriculum decisions are based on the analysis of these needs and on research, the expertise of the teachers, and the recommendations of learned societies.

- the design and delivery of professional development opportunities to meet the needs of all staff members to improve instruction for a specific purpose

- reflection on professional practice

Multiple opportunities to learn, which are aligned to the district's vision and mission, are provided to both staff and students. These educational opportunities are sensitive to and inclusive of the diverse student population. The types of professional development in place promote a focus on student learning consistent with the school vision and mission. The length of a student's day or year can be extended to provide the necessary time and instruction for success. Providing ongoing resources is a requirement to sustain the culture of the organization; it is the leader's role to secure these.

A positive disposition of teachers to their students enhances teachers' capacity to change the lives of their students. Believing all students can learn and all students are to be valued for their uniqueness contributes to their self-confidence and self-esteem; this belief, in turn, translates into more learning and greater success. Teachers know that "you get what you expect." If they expect the best, they will not be disappointed.

The effective leader is the key to an effective school culture.

The school leader models the very essence of behaviors expected from teachers and students. The leader's knowledge base, enthusiasm, skill, and modeling inspire others to achieve at high levels. The leader encourages and models life-long learning and striving for excellence. Nothing less than the best effort is what is expected every day in every way from every person.

Murphy (1998) states, "In schools where there is a strong professional culture, teachers and principals operate with an interdependent connected relationship" (p.365). The culture created through this relationship fosters the achievement of the school's ultimate mission, success for all students.

STANDARD 2: THE CULTURE OF TEACHING AND LEARNING

A school administrator is an educational leader who promotes the success of all students by advocating, nurturing, and sustaining a school culture and instructional program conducive to student learning and staff professional growth.

Component 2b: Developing and Sustaining the Culture — Component Performance Table

LEVEL OF PERFORMANCE			
Central Themes *	**Rudimentary**	**Developing**	**Proficient**	**Accomplished**
A Vision for Success	There is little or no evidence that the school leader is aware of the role of school environment and how it impacts the school's vision.	There is limited evidence that the school leader understands the kind of environment that contributes to the achievement of the school's vision.	There is clear evidence that the school leader has supported an environment that contributed to the achievement of the school's vision.	There is clear, convincing, and consistent evidence that the school leader has fostered the creation of an environment that directly and positively enhances the school's vision.
A Focus on Teaching and Learning	There is little or no evidence that the school leader has engaged teachers in activities to improve instruction or has established student achievement goals.	There is limited evidence that the school leader has provided teachers opportunities to engage in appropriate professional development activities that support the school vision or has established clearly defined achievement goals for all.	There is clear evidence that the school leader has provided teachers a variety of opportunities for professional growth that support the school vision and/or has established clear expectations for all.	There is clear, convincing, and consistent evidence that the school leader has created a learning community in which teachers are provided opportunities for appropriate professional growth and reflection that support the vision of the school and in which high exceptions are established for all.
An Involvement of all Stakeholders	There is little or no evidence that the school leader has involved stakeholders in any activity designed to support an effective instructional program and culture for teaching and learning.	There is limited evidence that the school leader has involved stakeholders in any activities that build an effective instructional program or culture for teaching and learning.	There is clear evidence that the school leader has created opportunities for various stakeholders to engage in and support an effective instructional program and culture for teaching and learning.	There is clear, convincing, and consistent evidence that the school leader has ensured that all appropriate stakeholders have a responsibility for and share in the planning, shaping, and implementation of an effective instructional program and culture for teaching and learning.
A Demonstration of Ethical Behavior	There is little or no evidence that the school leader has demonstrated integrity in the development of the instructional program and school culture that includes and ensures success for all students and staff in a fair and equitable way.	There is limited evidence that the school leader has demonstrated integrity and sensitivity to the needs of the diverse student population in the development of the instructional program and a school culture that is fair and equitable for all.	There is clear evidence that the school leader has demonstrated integrity in the creation of an effective instructional program and school culture that provides equitable opportunities for most students.	There is clear, convincing, and consistent evidence that the school leader has demonstrated integrity in ensuring that all aspects of the instructional program and school culture are sensitive to, and inclusive of, the diversity among the school population, and ensures that all students are actively represented in a fair and equitable way.

*These are the four central themes that unify the six Standards. They are fully described in Chapter 4 of this bo

Ensuring an Inclusive Culture

Effective school leaders will support and develop a school culture that is conducive to school learning. Only by the leaders' supporting collaboration with staff, parents, and citizens can effective and ongoing student learning occur. Improvement of student learning can only be achieved if the educational leader ensures an inclusive culture.

The key component to ensuring an inclusive culture is for the educational leader to focus professional development on student learning with the school's vision and goals. This will support a school culture of high expectations for students, staff, and the educational leader. Success of a strong professional development program will enhance the feeling of being valued by students and staff.

Recognizing accomplishments and successes of students, staff, and graduates can ensure an inclusive culture. By celebrating the successes of students, staff, and graduates with the school and community, the educational leader can provide role models for others to emulate. Valuing and recognizing the successes and accomplishments of the educational community support the culture and importance of learning.

The education program and school organized and aligned for success will assess the school culture and climate on a regular basis. Information and data from a variety of sources will be utilized to make decisions to sustain and improve the culture for student learning.

In my professional practice, ensuring an inclusive culture was essential in providing an environment for student learning. As an educational leader, I would continually assess the community, student body, and school staff to determine how the culture for student learning could be improved. Only by involving all participants can a school leader realize a collaborated effort and ensure student learning is improved.

Robert Buchanan, Ph.D.
Department of Educational Administration
Southern Missouri State University
Cape Girardeau, Missouri

"Success of a strong professional development program will enhance the feeling of being valued by students and staff."

An inclusive school culture is one in which the school leader ensures that all individuals are treated with fairness, dignity, and respect. An accomplished school leader must understand the value of diversity, the benefits it brings to a school community, and the ways in which these benefits must be translated into the educational program. Ethnic diversity, racial diversity, gender differences, as well as different learning styles and needs, must be considered. An effective school culture assures that all these factors have a bearing on the design of the instructional experiences for the students. Learning experiences must provide for the diverse needs of the children. The accomplished school leader identifies and removes barriers to student learning and creates a comprehensive instructional program for all students in which high expectations for all are valued. The school leader actively ensures that all the diverse groups in the community are represented in the decision-making process.

As a microcosm of our diverse society, the school must foster relationships built on trust, mutual respect, collaboration, and cooperation. These habits of character must become habits of mind and action for each member of the school community.

A safe and supportive learning environment is necessary for student comfort, risk-taking, and success. The school leader cannot tolerate behaviors that diminish any individual's capacity for success in the school community.

The terms "diversity" and "the diverse community" are frequently used in the Component Performance Table for 2c. These terms denote all factors that create diversity in the school and the community. Collectively, the terms refer to racial and ethnic diversity, diversity described by religion or gender, socioeconomic differences, differences in styles of learning, and all other factors that contribute to the makeup of the community.

Figure 6.7: Component 2c

STANDARD 2: THE CULTURE OF TEACHING AND LEARNING

A school administrator is an educational leader who promotes the success of all students by advocating, nurturing, and sustaining a school culture and instructional program conducive to student learning and staff professional growth.

Component 2c: Ensuring an Inclusive Culture — Component Performance Table

	LEVEL OF PERFORMANCE			
Central Themes *	**Rudimentary**	**Developing**	**Proficient**	**Accomplished**
A Vision for Success	There is little or no evidence that the school leader demonstrates any awareness of the diversity within the school community or provides any opportunities for students from diverse backgrounds to work toward a realization of the school's vision.	There is limited evidence that the school leader demonstrates an awareness of the diversity within the school community, or supports opportunities for students from diverse backgrounds to work toward a realization of the school's vision.	There is clear evidence that the school leader builds on the diversity within the school community and provides appropriate opportunities for students from diverse backgrounds to work toward a realization of the school's vision.	There is clear, convincing, and consistent evidence that the school leader is sensitive to the needs of all students, has created opportunities for students from diverse backgrounds to work toward the vision of the school, and has ensured that all students have access to these opportunities.
A Focus on Teaching and Learning	There is little or no evidence that the school leader is aware of any barriers to student learning or is sensitive to the individual needs of the diverse community.	There is limited evidence that the school leader has identified any barriers to learning, or has linked the barriers to the diversity within the community.	There is clear evidence that the school leader has identified barriers to learning, is sensitive to the needs of the diverse student population, and has had some success in removing each of these barriers.	There is clear, convincing, and consistent evidence that the school leader has identified barriers to learning that are insensitive to the needs of the diverse student population, has removed these barriers, and has facilitated the creation of a comprehensive instructional program for all students.
An Involvement of all Stakeholders	There is little or no evidence that stakeholders were involved in the process of creating an inclusive instructional program.	There is limited evidence that stakeholders were involved in the process of ensuring an inclusive instructional program and school culture.	There is clear evidence that the stakeholders assist the school leader in identifying most of the diversity within the community and help to include representatives in the decision-making process for some of the school's instructional programs.	There is clear, convincing and consistent evidence that the stakeholders assist the school leader in identifying the diversity within the community and help to include representatives from these groups in the decision-making process for the school's instructional programs to ensure the school is sensitive to the needs of the community.
A Demonstration of Ethical Behavior	There is little or no evidence that the school leader provides equal teaching and learning opportunities for all members of the diverse school community.	There is limited evidence that the school leader provides equal teaching and learning opportunities for most members of the diverse school community.	There is clear evidence that the school leader has provided equal teaching and learning opportunities for all members of the diverse school community and has established clear expectations for all.	There is clear, convincing, and consistent evidence that the school leader has actively ensured equal teaching and learning opportunities for all members of the diverse school community. Further, the leader has established clear expectations for all.

*These are the four central themes that unify the six Standards. They are fully described in Chapter 4 of this book.

Monitoring and Evaluating the Culture

When I consider the concept and practice of monitoring and evaluating the culture of student learning, I think of the many ways in which we as educators strive to change, update and improve the learning experience for all students. I ask my teachers and supervisors to do the same by reflecting on their practice, on professional literature, on their discussions with colleagues, and on the information derived from professional visits and attendance at workshops. Through these activities, I believe, I gain an appreciation for the efforts of the staff. As a building administrator, I find it important to keep in touch with students to better assess what they are learning and what they value in good teaching and learning.

Geoffrey R. Geiger, Assistant Principal
Toms River High School East
Toms River, New Jersey

In a school of excellence, the culture and climate of the school are assessed on a regular basis through student peer groups, informal teachers' leaders meetings, and surveys. A clear understanding of measurement, assessment, and evaluation strategies guides the school leader. Additionally, there is an ongoing assessment of both teacher and student performance.

The school leader provides the staff and students an opportunity to use multiple sources of data to evaluate the school climate. Feedback from parent and community surveys is used to make decisions regarding the school. The effectiveness of the work of the teaching staff is also monitored and evaluated on an ongoing basis. A variety of supervisory and differentiated evaluation models are employed. These models are respectful of the developmental needs of the teaching staff.

> *"... keep in touch with students to better assess what they are learning and what they value in good teaching and learning."*

Barriers to student learning are identified, classified, and addressed. The school leader acquires data on student academic progress on a continual basis. These data are from standardized tests, classroom performance grades and other information that might include year-end portfolios, anecdotal reports from teachers and parents, and other sources. The school leader uses this information to better understand how instructional effectiveness, curriculum alignment, environmental issues, or other factors impact student learning.

STANDARD 2: THE CULTURE OF TEACHING AND LEARNING

A school administrator is an educational leader who promotes the success of all students by advocating, nurturing, and sustaining a school culture and instructional program conducive to student learning and staff professional growth.

Component 2d: Monitoring and Evaluating the Culture — Component Performance Table

Central Themes *	Rudimentary	Developing	Proficient	Accomplished
A Vision for Success	There is little or no evidence that the school leader assesses the instructional program or school culture or the impact the instructional program or culture has on attaining the vision of the school.	There is limited evidence that the school leader has assessed the instructional program or school culture or links the instructional program or the school culture to the fulfillment of the school's vision; the evidence may be of an assessment limited in scope, depth, or accuracy.	There is clear evidence that the school leader has established a reliable system to assess the instructional program and the school culture and uses the information produced to promote the vision of the school.	There is clear, convincing, and consistent evidence that the school leader has established a thorough and ongoing assessment of the instructional program and the school culture and uses the information produced to promote the school vision.
A Focus on Teaching and Learning	There is little or no evidence that the school leader assesses teacher or student performance as a part of monitoring and evaluating the instructional program.	There is limited evidence that the school leader assesses teacher or student performance, or has made any link between instruction and student achievement.	There is clear evidence that the school leader has created a system of periodically appraising teacher and student performance and that this information is usually used to inform instructional decisions.	There is clear, convincing, and consistent evidence that the school leader has created an ongoing system of appraising teacher and student performance and that this information is systematically used to inform instructional decisions throughout the school year.
An Involvement of all Stakeholders	There is little or no evidence that the school leader involves stakeholders in providing or analyzing data related to the instructional program or culture of learning.	There is limited evidence that the school leader involves some stakeholders with an opportunity to provide or analyze data about the instructional program or culture of learning.	There is clear evidence that the school leader involves stakeholders in a variety of ways to provide and analyze data about the instructional program and culture of learning on a regular basis.	There is clear, convincing, and consistent evidence that the school leader gives stakeholders responsibility for gathering and analyzing information related to the instructional program and culture of learning throughout the school year, and gives them an active role in using this information to share in decisions about school improvement.
A Demonstration of Ethical Behavior	There is little or no evidence that the school leader demonstrates any integrity in providing the school community information about the evaluation of the school's instructional program and culture.	There is limited evidence that the school leader demonstrates integrity in providing the community information about the evaluation of the school's instructional program and culture.	There is clear evidence that the school leader has created a system for monitoring and evaluating the instructional program and culture that is open and honest. Further, the leader provides information about the evaluation of the instructional program and culture periodically.	There is clear, convincing, and consistent evidence that the school leader has created a system for monitoring and evaluating the instructional program and culture that is thorough, open and honest. Further, the leader ensures that information about the instructional program and culture is provided on an ongoing basis, in a variety of formats, to ensure understanding by all members of the diverse community.

*These are the four central themes that unify the six Standards. They are fully described in Chapter 4 of this b

A school administrator is an educational leader who promotes the success of all students by ensuring management of the organization, operations, and resources for a safe, efficient, and effective learning environment (CCSSO, 1996, p. 14).

STANDARD

The purpose of this Standard is to improve student learning through the effective, efficient, and equitable use of all types of resources. Management decisions are made based on complete knowledge of learning, teaching, and student development. The school leader must use knowledge of organizations to create an effective learning environment that enhances the success of every student. Resources such as personnel, facilities, funding, technology, and equipment enhance an effective learning climate. Operational procedures, rules, and policies are established to maintain school safety and security and to increase student academic achievement. Management decisions regarding human resources, fiscal operations, use of facilities and space, legal issues, time management and scheduling, technology, and equipment should be based on sound organizational practice. Monitoring and evaluation of operational systems ensure that leaders work responsibly and effectively to enhance student learning and demonstrate accountability of the school and district to the community. Skill in job analysis, supervision, recruitment, selection, and appraisal for staff positions, as well as background in collective bargaining, strengthens the leader's use of personnel resources to further student achievement. Effective administrators define job roles, assign tasks, delegate appropriately, and require accountability. The educational leader not only relies on regular tax assessments but also actively seeks additional sources of financial, human, and physical supports. The involvement of stakeholders ensures that management and operational decisions take into consideration the needs of several audiences, while at the same time focusing the entire community on student achievement as the ultimate target. To include stakeholders in management decisions, educational leaders need skill in conflict resolution, consensus building, group processes, and effective communication (National Policy Board of Education Administration).

Each Standard is framed by areas of focus defined by knowledge and skills, which may be evidenced at different levels of performance as indicated on the accompanying rubric tables. These areas of focus may be applied in different ways on the rubric tables. The leadership position (e.g., principal, superintendent, etc.) and context (e.g., elementary, secondary, urban, suburban, etc.) will determine their use.

STANDARD 3: THE MANAGEMENT OF LEARNING

Areas of Focus	Knowledge and Skills
Organization	▨ uses knowledge of learning, teaching, student development, and organizational development to optimize learning for all students ▨ applies appropriate models and principles of organizational development and management, including data-based decision-making with indicators of equity, effectiveness, and efficiency to optimize learning for all students
Operations	▨ involves stakeholders in operations and setting priorities ▨ uses appropriate and effective communication and group processing skills to build consensus and resolve conflict in order to link resources to the instructional vision ▨ models community collaboration for staff and offers opportunities for staff to develop family and community collaboration skills
Resources	▨ uses problem-solving skills and knowledge of strategic, long-range operational planning for effective, efficient, and equitable resource allocation and alignment ▨ seeks new resources to facilitate learning ▨ applies and assesses current technologies for school management, business procedures, and scheduling
Safe Schools	▨ assures safe, effective, and efficient facilities planning and use

Making Management Decisions to Ensure Successful Teaching and Learning

As principal for over a quarter of a century and now as a professor in educational administration, I believe that making managerial decisions to ensure successful teaching and learning starts with the leader's perspective and the anticipation of school wide ramifications when these decisions involve educational choices. A safe, efficient, and effective learning environment can be achieved successfully only when the principal demonstrates knowledge of learning, teaching, and student development to make uniform management decisions. Knowing how to balance a stable educational program while providing opportunities requires a set of guidelines derived from standards.

Dr. Clarence Golden
Frostburg State University
Frostburg, Maryland

Schools are very complex, with multiple and often conflicting sets of expectations, needs, values, and priorities. Making management decisions in such complex settings involves identifying, clarifying, and resolving competing needs, forces, and claims of all stakeholders involved. The overriding goal of management decision-making is meeting the mission of the school and supporting a successful teaching and learning program. When conflicts emerge, the question one might ask is, "What solution will best work for the success of all students?"

As a base for decision-making, the school leader relies on two kinds of theoretical knowledge: knowledge of principles and theories of effective organization and knowledge of components of successful teaching and learning programs. With this base, the school leader works to establish a proactive, rather than reactive, process for decision-making. Doing so requires problem identification and problem-solving skills, and a clear reliance on group process and consensus building that involves all stakeholders. After regularly reviewing all teacher and student data, the leader analyzes this information to inform and enhance the teaching and learning process.

Effective decision-making does not begin with predetermined answers or solutions. It begins with identification of needs, questions, issues, priorities, and "givens." For example, in effective schools the use of technology is framed as an answer to a set of questions about effective teaching, learning, and management, not as a previously established solution to what may be unclearly defined needs.

> *"Knowing how to balance a stable educational program while providing opportunities requires a set of guidelines derived from standards."*

The effective leader assumes an ethical stance in conceptualizing and facilitating management decision-making. The leader is willing to take risks, and is equally willing to accept responsibility for the consequences of those risks. Management decisions are made using all available data that attempt to consider the best interests of all stakeholders. Trusting other people's judgment, opinions, and values, the leader provides an open and safe arena for their proper consideration, and builds a trustful environment for shared decision-making. The leader assures that the contractual and other legal rights and responsibilities of all concerned are taken into consideration.

STANDARD 3: THE MANAGEMENT OF LEARNING

A school administrator is an educational leader who promotes the success of all students by ensuring management of the organization, operations, and resources for a safe, efficient, and effective learning environment.

Component 3a: Making Management Decisions to Ensure Successful Teaching and Learning — Component Performance Table

	LEVEL OF PERFORMANCE			
Central Themes *	**Rudimentary**	**Developing**	**Proficient**	**Accomplished**
A Vision for Success	There is little or no evidence that the school leader makes management decisions that are linked to the school's vision.	There is limited evidence that the school leader considers the school's vision when making management decisions.	There is clear evidence that the school leader makes most management decisions in a way that supports the school's vision.	There is clear, convincing, and consistent evidence that, on an ongoing basis, the school leader makes all management decisions in a way that promotes the school's vision.
A Focus on Teaching and Learning	There is little or no evidence that the school leader demonstrates any awareness of learning, teaching, and student development to inform management decisions.	There is limited evidence that the school leader demonstrates any understanding of learning, teaching, and student development to inform management decisions or rarely uses this information to enhance teaching and learning.	There is clear evidence that the school leader demonstrates an understanding of learning, teaching, and student development to inform most management decisions and frequently uses this information to enhance teaching and learning.	There is clear, convincing, and consistent evidence that the school leader demonstrates an understanding of learning, teaching, and student development to inform all management decisions and continuously uses this information to enhance teaching and learning.
An Involvement of all Stakeholders	There is little or no evidence that the school leader involves stakeholders in the management decision-making process.	There is limited evidence that the school leader makes appropriate use of stakeholders in the management decision-making process.	There is clear evidence that the school leader at times involves appropriate stakeholders in the management decision-making process.	There is clear, convincing, and consistent evidence that the school leader actively recruits and involves appropriate stakeholders in the management decision-making process on an ongoing basis.
A Demonstration of Ethical Behavior	There is little or no evidence that the school leader has ever employed ethical principles in the decision-making process that ensure fairness and equity for all.	There is limited evidence that the school leader has employed ethical principles in the decision-making process that ensure fairness and equity for all.	There is clear evidence that the school leader employs ethical principles in the decision-making process and attempts to ensure fairness and equity for all.	There is clear, convincing, and consistent evidence that the school leader employs ethical principles in the decision-making process and ensures fairness and equity for all.

*These are the four central themes that unify the six Standards. They are fully described in Chapter 4 of this book

Developing Procedures to Ensure Successful Teaching and Learning

If a school is to be effective in its goal to provide a quality education for all students, the principal must be empowered and unencumbered to monitor and evaluate the processes of teaching and learning daily.

In an effort to install precise, effective, and easy-to-understand procedures for monitoring the teaching and learning processes, the modern day principal should encourage teacher collaboration. Such collegiality will provide a forum in which academic goals can be determined based on student needs. Methods for equitably evaluating teacher effectiveness can also be agreed upon and implemented.

My experience as a high school principal for twelve years has been that this sincere openness of communication will result in a viable and easy-to-understand set of procedures, which will strategically increase teachers' confidence in and ownership of their destinies.

The principal of the 21st Century must understand that through collaboration with all stakeholders, a school's atmosphere can undergo a metamorphosis. The resulting transformation will be a friendly, caring, family-oriented organization in which every contributing individual will work as a team member in reaching the common goal of educating all students.

Dr. Tom Clark
Picayune District Office
Picayune, Mississippi

Two maxims from the ISLLC Standards clearly spell out the overriding guidelines for developing procedures:

- Operational procedures are designed and managed to maximize opportunities for successful learning.

- Operational plans and procedures to achieve the vision and goals of the school are in place.

In schools characterized by the above maxims, the development of procedures, like the decision-making process, is proactive rather than reactive. "What are all the factors that actually or potentially might affect the smooth and successful implementation of our instructional program?" is a question that might typically frame the process. "When these factors compete or conflict," the questioning might continue, "how might they best be analyzed, clarified, and resolved to support the development of effective procedures?"

Because schools are complex, they require a complex set of procedures. The set might typically include procedures that address:

- School improvement and curriculum review/revision

- Development and modification of teacher and student schedules

- Budget-making, revising, and monitoring

- Community use of facilities

- Monitoring and reporting student progress to parents and community

- Staff evaluation and professional development

- Information flow to staff, students, and community

- Student, parent, and staff rights, responsibilities, and needs

- Conflict resolution between and among students, staff, parents, and community

- Ongoing monitoring of effective and legal use of all resources

In developing procedures for these and other aspects of school governance, there are questions that are helpful to guide and monitor the process:

Is this procedure fair, equitable, reasonable, workable, sensitive, and legally defensible?

Who is going to develop,implement, and monitor this procedure?

What consequences are explicit or implicit in the implementation of this procedure?

What are the direct and indirect costs of this procedure?

Ultimately, how will this procedure maximize opportunities for successful learning?

Like all other aspects of school governance, developing procedures is an inclusive process, involving all stakeholders. Like other aspects, it is a recursive process involving periodic review and revision. And, like other aspects, successful development and implementation of procedures requires an effective communication system. All those involved need to know of opportunities in the development of procedures and to also know the details of the procedures themselves. Additionally they need to know how procedures can ultimately affect them, and know what recourse they have if procedures are inappropriate.

> "The principal of the 21st Century must understand that through collaboration with all stakeholders, a school's atmosphere can undergo a metamorphosis."

Effective school leaders are human, subject to complex and often weighty pressures, needs, and requirements, and guided by their own visions, hopes, and dreams for a successful school. In the complex world in which they operate, school leaders may well be advised to have a personal set of procedures to monitor their own lives. These procedures might well include time to take stock of "how they are" physically, mentally, and emotionally. These procedures might well include prescribed time for reflection.

Am I responding to pressures with some perspective?

Am I placing teaching and learning first?

Am I building in time for myself as an individual — to grow, to relax, and to think?

Am I the kind of school leader I used to dream I would become?

STANDARD 3: THE MANAGEMENT OF LEARNING

A school administrator is an educational leader who promotes the success of all students by ensuring management of the organization, operations, and resources for a safe, efficient, and effective learning environment.

Component 3b: Developing Procedures to Ensure Successful Teaching and Learning — Component Performance Table

	LEVEL OF PERFORMANCE			
Central Themes *	**Rudimentary**	**Developing**	**Proficient**	**Accomplished**
A Vision for Success	There is little or no evidence that the school leader facilitates the development of any procedures for successful teaching and learning linked to the school's vision.	There is limited evidence that the school leader considers the school's vision when facilitating the development of procedures for successful teaching and learning.	There is clear evidence that the school leader facilitates the development of most procedures for successful teaching and learning to support the school's vision.	There is clear, convincing, and consistent evidence that the school leader collaborates with stakeholders to develop, assess, and improve procedures for successful teaching and learning to ensure the support of the school's vision.
A Focus on Teaching and Learning	There is little or no evidence that the school leader is aware of any emerging trends or has facilitated the development of any procedures or policies to support teaching and learning.	There is limited evidence that the school leader recognizes any emerging trends to facilitate the development of school procedures and policies that are connected to the teaching and learning process.	There is clear evidence that the school leader recognizes, studies, and applies some emerging trends to facilitate the development of school procedures and policies that support and enhance the teaching and learning process.	There is clear, convincing, and consistent evidence that the school leader recognizes, studies, and applies emerging trends to facilitate the development of school procedures and policies that effectively support and enhance the teaching and learning process on an ongoing basis.
An Involvement of all Stakeholders	There is little or no evidence that the school leader involves any stakeholders in the development of procedures to ensure successful teaching and learning.	There is limited evidence that the school leader involves appropriate stakeholders in the development of school procedures to ensure successful teaching and learning.	There is clear evidence that the school leader involves stakeholders in developing many of the school procedures to ensure successful teaching and learning.	There is clear, convincing, and consistent evidence that the school leader actively engages appropriate stakeholders in developing all school procedures that ensure successful teaching and learning.
A Demonstration of Ethical Behavior	There is little or no evidence that the school leader demonstrates integrity in facilitating the development of any procedures that support teaching and learning which are fair and equitable to all.	There is limited evidence that the school leader demonstrates integrity in facilitating the development of some procedures that support teaching and learning which are fair and equitable to all.	There is clear evidence that the school leader demonstrates integrity in facilitating the development of most procedures that support teaching and learning which are fair and equitable to all.	There is clear, convincing, and consistent evidence that the school leader demonstrates integrity in facilitating the development of all procedures that support teaching and learning which are fair and equitable to all.

*These are the four central themes that unify the six Standards. They are fully described in Chapter 4 of this book

Allocating Resources to Ensure Successful Teaching and Learning

If missions are to be achieved and visions realized, it is necessary for school leaders to align their words and actions. It is imperative for leaders to preserve precious resources and to make every effort to utilize them to support teaching and learning.

At Johns Hopkins, aspiring educational leaders in either the Masters of Science Degree or Certificate Programs in Administration and Supervision are provided with the theories, best practices, and real life situations which emphasize this alignment of resources and the all important outcome of student success. As applicable, scenario-based instruction linked to the Interstate School Leaders Licensure Consortium Standards has become an integral means for applying theory and practice to the allocation of resources.

James R. McGowan, Ph.D.
Senior Faculty and Program Coordinator
Johns Hopkins University
Columbia, Maryland

Perhaps in no arena of school governance is the need to confront conflicting needs, desires, claims, values, and realities stronger than in the allocation of resources. It is a rare school leader who has not said, "There just isn't enough. . ." And the sentence can end with any of a wide variety of resources: money, time, facilities, personnel. . . and the list goes on. The school leader faces this dilemma in two ways: being aggressive in seeking additional resources and overseeing a process to allocate the resources at hand.

How does the effective school leader resolve the conflicts inherent in allocating resources? First, by holding always as the central guideline the questions: "What is best for teaching and learning?" and "What will best help us meet our goals and achieve our mission?"

> *"It is imperative for leaders to preserve precious resources and to make every effort to utilize them to support teaching and learning."*

Then, the allocation of resources depends, as do all areas of governance, upon an inclusive process that involves stakeholders in the process of identifying needs, establishing priorities, weighing possibilities and consequences, and establishing a system of responsibility and accountability. The inclusive nature of the process for allocating resources rests upon a fundamental tenet that all must consider: the resources of the school belong to all the stakeholders; they are not the exclusive domain of any individuals or special interest groups. All stakeholders entrust to their representatives who are the decision-makers the responsibility for the development of a resource allocation plan that is thoughtful, equitable, comprehensive, and legally defensible.

A responsible resource allocation plan includes a clear system of monitoring and accountability. Because the resources are public, so, too, must be the reporting of the use of those resources. The realities are that problems occur, unexpected needs arise, emergencies happen, and priorities shift. But as these contingencies are met, if the allocation of resources is reevaluated, that process, the reasons for it, and the outcome must be public.

Figure 6.11: Component 3c

STANDARD 3: THE MANAGEMENT OF LEARNING

A school administrator is an educational leader who promotes the success of all students by ensuring management of the organization, operations, and resources for a safe, efficient, and effective learning environment.

Component 3c: Allocating Resources to Ensure Successful Teaching and Learning — Component Performance Table

	LEVEL OF PERFORMANCE			
Central Themes *	**Rudimentary**	**Developing**	**Proficient**	**Accomplished**
A Vision for Success	There is little or no evidence that the school leader effectively uses resources to promote the vision of the school.	There is limited evidence that the school leader makes all decisions regarding the allocation of resources with appropriate consideration of the school's vision.	There is clear evidence that the school leader effectively and fairly allocates most school resources in a way that supports the school's vision.	There is clear, convincing, and consistent evidence that the school leader ensures that all available resources are allocated effectively and fairly in a way that supports the school's vision.
A Focus on Teaching and Learning	There is little or no evidence that the school leader uses resources effectively or efficiently, and/or considers the relationship of these resources to successful teaching and learning.	There is limited evidence that the school leader makes decisions regarding the allocation of resources based on a consideration of the link between the allocation of these resources and how they support successful teaching and learning.	There is clear evidence that the school leader makes routine decisions related to the effective allocation and use of resources in support of successful teaching and learning.	There is clear, convincing, and consistent evidence that the school leader has developed creative ways to obtain, allocate, and conserve resources to support successful teaching and learning.
An Involvement of all Stakeholders	There is little or no evidence that the school leader is aware of the stakeholders' interests or provides them any forum to express their opinion on how resources are to be allocated.	There is limited evidence that the school leader provides stakeholders an opportunity to express their opinion about the allocation of resources, or uses this information to support allocation decisions.	There is clear evidence that the school leader is sensitive to the competing interests of the various school groups and includes some stakeholders in most of the decision-making related to resource allocation.	There is clear, convincing, and consistent evidence that the school leader is sensitive to the competing interests of various school groups and collaboratively engages appropriate stakeholders in all decisions related to resource allocation.
A Demonstration of Ethical Behavior	There is little or no evidence to suggest that the school leader demonstrates integrity in allocating resources to support teaching and learning in a fair and equitable way.	There is limited evidence that the school leader demonstrates integrity in allocating resources to support teaching and learning in a fair and equitable way.	There is clear evidence that the school leader demonstrates integrity in allocating most resources to support teaching and learning in a fair and equitable manner.	There is clear, convincing, and consistent evidence that the school leader always demonstrates integrity in allocating all resources to support teaching and learning in a fair and equitable way.

*These are the four central themes that unify the six Standards. They are fully described in Chapter 4 of this book.

COMPONENT THREE D

Creating a Safe, Healthy Environment to Ensure Successful Teaching and Learning

*It is the belief of the Palisades School District that this component, Creating a Safe, Healthy Environment to Ensure Successful Teaching and Learning, is the foundation for all the other components in the ISLLC Standards. We focus on ensuring this in each of our schools. Until students feel safe, no learning will take place. Creating a safe and healthy school environment is essential to ensure successful teaching and learning. All members of the school community need to feel safe before they can be open to learning. **Safety** and **respect** are two reasonable requests we have for each other in the Palisades School District. This expectation is for all members of the larger school community. It begins with the interpersonal relationship between teacher and child in each classroom and spreads out to all our connections with the broader school community. When students feel safe and know that we truly care about them and their success, they will do anything to become successful.*

We believe if we are respectful of each other, then everyone will always be safe.

Francis V. Barnes, Ph.D., Superintendent
Palisades School District
Kintnersville, Pennsylvania

The physical and emotional safety and health of every staff member and student are critical to the achievement of the goal that all students will succeed. Teachers cannot teach effectively nor can students learn and perform successfully in an environment that does not support and protect their safety and health.

The creation and maintenance of such an environment is the responsibility of all stakeholders under the guidance and direction of effective school leaders. The physical and emotional well-being of staff and students is nurtured in an environment that is fully responsive to laws and regulations governing safety and health. Particular attention is paid to meeting the needs of anyone in the school — student, staff member, or parent — who has physical conditions requiring special provisions.

The safety of all is addressed through a clear and rigorously enforced set of rules and procedures including those addressing both routine and emergency conditions. Safety, both physical and emotional, is addressed by considerations of space and traffic flow; those responsible for these aspects of a school realize that crowding often causes tension and actual danger, and they work to reduce tension and danger through effective management of space.

"Until students feel safe, no learning will take place. "

Emotional safety is no less important in a school than is physical safety. Students and staff have a right to an environment free from factors that impinge on emotional safety: harassment, teasing, embarrassment, or prejudice. Effective schools are marked by environments that build a sense of the worth and dignity of self and others. The school leader works with all concerned to build such environments.

These environments proudly reflect the values of the school and the school community. An aesthetically pleasing physical plant and displays, symbols, and rituals reflecting the work and values of the school all provide a setting in which all students feel comfortable and of which they can be proud. In such a setting, all students are free to succeed.

CHAPTER 6

STANDARD 3: THE MANAGEMENT OF LEARNING

A school administrator is an educational leader who promotes the success of all students by ensuring management of the organization, operations, and resources for a safe, efficient, and effective learning environment.

Component 3d: Creating a Safe, Healthy Environment to Ensure Successful Teaching and Learning — Component Performance Table

Central Themes *	LEVEL OF PERFORMANCE			
	Rudimentary	**Developing**	**Proficient**	**Accomplished**
A Vision for Success	There is little or no evidence that the school leader is aware of unsafe or unhealthy conditions in the school or has attempted to ensure a safe and healthy environment that can support the school's vision.	There is limited evidence that the school leader is aware of health and safety-related issues existing in the school, or works to create a school environment to support the school's vision.	There is clear evidence that the school leader creates a school environment that supports the school's vision, and periodically identifies and addresses most unsafe and unhealthy conditions in the school.	There is clear, convincing, and consistent evidence that the school leader continuously creates a social, physical, and emotional environment that promotes the school's vision and identifies and addresses unsafe and unhealthy conditions in the school.
A Focus on Teaching and Learning	There is little or no evidence that the school leader makes plans for a safe and healthy environment to ensure successful teaching and learning or addresses safety concerns as they arise.	There is limited evidence that the school leader creates a safe school either in planning or in actions.	There is clear evidence that the school leader creates an environment that is generally conducive to ensure effective teaching and learning, although there may be areas that are exceptions.	Clear, convincing, and consistent evidence exists that the school leader ensures the creation of an environment conducive to successful teaching and learning for all.
An Involvement of all Stakeholders	There is little or no evidence that the school leader has made an attempt to address the issue of safe schools with any stakeholders or to enlist their support in creating an environment conducive to teaching and learning.	There is limited evidence that the school leader attempts to address the issue of safe schools with some stakeholders, and/or that the leader is aware of local community agencies that could assist the school to create an effective, safe learning environment.	There is clear evidence that the school leader addresses the issue of safe schools with appropriate stakeholders and involves some community agencies to provide the school services to create an effective, safe learning environment.	There is clear, convincing, and consistent evidence that the school leader addresses the issue of safe schools with appropriate stakeholders and fosters and develops partnerships with community agencies to create an effective, safe learning environment.
A Demonstration of Ethical Behavior	There is little or no evidence that the school leader treats people fairly and equitably in the application of the laws and procedures designed to protect the health and safety of all.	There is limited evidence that the school leader treats people fairly and equitably in the application of some of the laws and procedures designed to protect the health and safety of all.	There is clear evidence that the school leader treats people fairly and equitably in the application of the laws and procedures designed to protect the health and safety of all.	There is clear, convincing, and consistent evidence that the school leader treats people fairly and equitably in the application of all laws and procedures designed to protect the health and safety of all and is an advocate for the physical, social, and emotional well-being of all members of the school community.

*These are the four central themes that unify the six Standards. They are fully described in Chapter 4 of this boo

A school administrator is an educational leader who promotes the success of all students by collaborating with families and community members, responding to diverse community interests and needs, and mobilizing community resources (CCSSO, 1996, p. 16).

STANDARD

The purpose of this Standard is to demonstrate that interaction with and support by the school and district communities are essential to the success of educational leaders as well as their students. Administrators must see schools as an integral part of the larger community. Following that precept, collaboration and communication with families, businesses, governmental agencies, social service organizations, the media, and higher education institutions become critical to effective schooling. Examining emerging issues and trends that potentially impact the school and district will assist administrators to plan successful instructional programs and services. Assessing conditions and dynamics of the diverse school and district communities enables the educational leader to meet the needs of both students and the community. Working with the community to develop relevant and needed services, the school leader uses data on the following:

- students and staff

- the school environment

- family and community values, expectations, and priorities

- national and global conditions affecting schools

Effective and appropriate communications, coupled with involvement of families and other stakeholders in decisions, helps to ensure the continued support of those entities. Family involvement increases their children's learning. Seeing families as partners in the education of their youngsters, and believing that families have the best interests of their children in mind, helps the educational leader to involve them in decisions at the school and district levels.

Family and student issues that negatively impact student learning will be addressed through the collaboration of community agencies that integrate health, social, and other services. Good relationships with community leaders and outreach to different business, religious, political, and service agencies allow the school and district and the community-at-large to share resources and serve one another. Demonstrating the belief that diversity enriches the school and district lends credence to individuals and groups whose values and opinions may conflict. Providing leadership to programs serving students with special and exceptional needs further communicates to both internal and external audiences the importance of diversity. To work with all elements of the community, educational leaders must recognize, value, and communicate effectively with various cultural, ethnic, racial, and special interest groups. Modeling community collaboration for staff, and then offering opportunities for staff to develop collaborative skills, will maximize the points of contact between the schools and the community (National Policy Board of Education Administration).

Each Standard is framed by areas of focus defined by knowledge and skills, which may be evidenced at different levels of performance as indicated on the accompanying rubric tables. These areas of focus may be applied in different ways on the rubric tables. The leadership position (e.g., principal, superintendent, etc.) and context (e.g., elementary, secondary, urban, suburban, etc.) will determine their use.

STANDARD 4: RELATIONSHIPS WITH THE BROADER COMMUNITY TO FOSTER LEARNING

Areas of Focus	Knowledge and Skills
Collaboration	<ul><li>applies comprehensive community relations models</li><li>uses effective marketing strategies and processes</li><li>develops outreach programs with different religious, business, political, and service groups</li><li>establishes partnerships with business, community, government, and higher education groups</li><li>involves stakeholders in the decision-making process</li><li>supports the belief that families have the best interest of their children in mind and involves families to impact student learning positively</li><li>collaborates with community agencies to integrate health, social, and other services</li></ul>
Community Interests and Needs	<ul><li>maintains high visibility and active involvement with the community</li><li>acknowledges individuals and groups and can analyze their perspectives</li></ul>
Community Resources	<ul><li>appropriately utilizes community resources, including youth services, to support student achievement, solve school problems, and achieve school goals</li><li>looks for opportunities to offer school resources to serve the community and social service agencies</li><li>uses public resources and funds appropriately and effectively</li></ul>
Diversity	<ul><li>capitalizes on the diversity of the school community to improve school programs and meet diverse needs of all students</li><li>serves as an advocate for students with special and exceptional needs</li></ul>

Understanding Community Needs

When I took the position of principal, it didn't take me long to realize that the school and the community were not "connected." In order to better understand the needs of all students, we began to involve the community in decisions affecting the school. We strengthened the parent/teacher organization and invited community members into the school to hear suggestions and gather information. School representatives went out into the community, as well. As a result of these efforts to understand the community's needs, I believe that we better served our students' needs and gained the community's confidence.

Douglas J. Bohrer, Principal (Retired)
Wall Intermediate School
Wall Township, New Jersey

Effective school leaders are sensitive to the fact that they must have a deep and broad understanding of the needs of the community before they can fully engage members of the community in the support of the school. The community and all its members play a crucial role in shaping and supporting the school. In this regard, all these members have needs — sometimes clearly defined and sometimes felt, but, as yet, unexpressed — to which the school leader wisely attends. These needs, whether they be economic, social, cultural, or related to some other issue, affect the way the community members view the school and the value the school has, if any, on satisfying these needs. The school leader must also understand that these needs are not static, but, in fact, they change over time. The school leader must, therefore, continually assess community needs and develop the ability to identify and predict patterns that are supported by data from these assessments. The effective leader then uses this information to modify, inform, and validate the vision of the school and to make decisions on teaching strategies that will foster learning and improve student achievement. There are several sources of data that can contribute to the leader's knowledge of community needs. Some of these sources might include:

- Community surveys conducted by the school

- Census data about changes in the community population

- News reports about changes in the community environment that might impact community members (e.g., the closing or creation of a business, economic changes)

- Results of recent local elections, including those that impact school funding or change the composition of the Board of Education

The effective school leader can and should enlist the support of stakeholders in this data collection effort. By collaborating with appropriate stakeholders on an ongoing basis, the leader can maximize the efficiency of the collection and analysis of these data and will be sure not only to ask the right questions, but also to ask the right people.

> "As a result of these efforts to understand the community's needs, ... we better served our students' needs and gained the community's confidence."

Finally, the effective school leader knows that the information collected about the needs of the community is done to enhance learning and promote the success of all students. This information must not be used inappropriately to advance anyone's or any group's personal gain. The leader will increase community support for this effort if community members are assured that the leader is acting for the central purpose of promoting the success of all students.

STANDARD 4: RELATIONSHIPS WITH THE BROADER COMMUNITY TO FOSTER LEARNING

A school administrator is an educational leader who promotes the success of all students by collaborating with families and community members, responding to diverse community interests and needs, and mobilizing community resources.

Component 4a: Understanding Community Needs — Component Performance Table

	LEVEL OF PERFORMANCE			
Central Themes *	**Rudimentary**	**Developing**	**Proficient**	**Accomplished**
A Vision for Success	There is little or no evidence that the school leader understands the needs of the community and how these needs could be reflected in the vision of the school.	There is limited evidence that the school leader attempts to understand the needs of the community, or that these needs are reflected in the vision of the school.	There is clear evidence that the school leader assesses the needs of the community and that patterns that emerge from these data are used to inform the vision of the school.	There is clear, convincing, and consistent evidence that the school leader assesses the needs of the community on an ongoing basis, has had the ability to identify and predict patterns that are supported by these data, and uses this information to modify, inform, and validate the vision of the school.
A Focus on Teaching and Learning	There is little or no evidence that the school leader assesses the needs of the community to provide data to inform effective teaching strategies that would foster learning.	There is limited evidence that the school leader assesses the needs of the community, or that resulting data were used by the leader to inform teaching strategies that would foster learning.	There is clear evidence that the school leader assesses the needs of the community and usually uses resulting data to modify teaching strategies that foster learning.	There is clear, convincing, and consistent evidence that the school leader assesses the needs of the community on an ongoing basis and continually uses resulting data to inform teaching strategies that clearly foster learning and improve student achievement.
An Involvement of all Stakeholders	There is little or no evidence that the school leader engages the assistance or support of stakeholders in assessing the needs of the community to foster learning in the school.	There is limited evidence that the school leader engages the assistance of some stakeholders in assessing the needs of the community with a goal of fostering learning in the school.	There is clear evidence that the school leader collaborates from time to time with some stakeholders in collecting and analyzing data concerning the needs of the community with a goal of fostering learning in the school.	There is clear, convincing, and consistent evidence that the school leader collaborates with appropriate stakeholders on an ongoing basis to collect and analyze data on the needs of the community with a goal of fostering learning in the school.
A Demonstration of Ethical Behavior	There is little or no evidence that the school leader demonstrates appreciation for and sensitivity to the needs and prevailing values of the diverse school community.	There is limited evidence that the school leader demonstrates appreciation for and/or sensitivity to the needs and prevailing values of the diverse school community.	There is clear evidence that the school leader frequently demonstrates appreciation for and/or sensitivity to the needs and prevailing values of the diverse school community.	There is clear, convincing, and consistent evidence that the school leader demonstrates appreciation for and sensitivity to the needs and prevailing values of the diverse school community on an ongoing basis.

*These are the four central themes that unify the six Standards. They are fully described in Chapter 4 of this bo

Involving Members of the Community

As a university professor I utilize the ISLLC Standards as a guide in providing effective training for prospective school leaders. These leaders must become knowledgeable of and develop strong dispositions on the interdependence of educational organizations in an open system. These leaders must develop an understanding of the accountability involved in addressing the transformational process and the involvement of stakeholders as active participants in the school in which they are expected to generate productive citizens. I ensure that our leadership preparation program provides many opportunities for students to interact with stakeholders during classes, seminars, and internships and through self-discovery approaches such as problem-based learning exercises and case studies. This type of training effectively prepares school leaders who will be empowered to employ both internal and external collaboration in promoting the success of all students.

LaVerne B. Allen, Ph.D.
Jackson State University
Jackson, Mississippi

Effective school leaders understand the importance of involving appropriate members of the community to support the success of all students. These leaders understand that schools clearly do not exist in isolation, but that their schools must be inextricably linked with the families of the students and the community they serve. Schools are, and must be, a vital part of the communities in which they are found, and effective school leaders involve both families and the larger community in all aspects of the education of students.

High performing school leaders have created effective, multifaceted strategies for collaborating with families and appropriate community members in ways that promote the school's vision and that contribute to effective teaching and learning activities. These leaders provide representatives of the community opportunities to come into the school throughout the year to engage in meaningful events and activities.

At the same time, the school leader encourages members of the school community to go into the community-at-large to engage in activities designed to enhance and supplement classroom instruction. For instance, teachers are encouraged to conduct field trips to local businesses, industries, or cultural centers to supplement classroom experiences and help students link their learning to real world applications.

The effective leader knows that establishing these community relationships cannot be done without assistance. Wise leaders are creative in ways of enlisting the assistance of a variety of stakeholders to reach out to groups beyond the school to strengthen these community ties.

Finally, the school leader must make it abundantly clear that there is no other motivation for creating these community relationships than to promote the success of all the students. It must be evident that these ties are not created for the personal benefit of the leader or any special group within the school or community. Failure to heed this advice could undermine all the efforts of the school leader in creating these important relationships.

Figure 6.14: Component 4b

STANDARD 4: RELATIONSHIPS WITH THE BROADER COMMUNITY TO FOSTER LEARNING

A school administrator is an educational leader who promotes the success of all students by collaborating with families and community members, responding to diverse community interests and needs, and mobilizing community resources.

Component 4b: Involving Members of the Community — Component Performance Table

Central Themes *	LEVEL OF PERFORMANCE			
	Rudimentary	Developing	Proficient	Accomplished
A Vision for Success	There is little or no evidence that the school leader demonstrates any understanding of, or an interest in, what is needed to involve members of the community in achieving the school vision.	The school leader demonstrates an understanding of the issues and challenges in engaging the school community in achieving the school vision or engages any significant segments of the community in this activity.	There is clear evidence that the school leader has a basic plan to engage the community to assist the school in achieving its vision. The plan generally addresses the issues and challenges to be faced in working toward the vision, and involves most appropriate stakeholders.	There is clear, convincing, and consistent evidence that the school leader has an effective, multifaceted plan for collaborating with families and community members in a way that contributes to the success of the school's vision. The plan's strategies address the issues and challenges to be faced in working toward the vision, and involve all appropriate stakeholders.
A Focus on Teaching and Learning	There is little or no evidence that the school leader plans for any partnerships between the school and community that will enhance or support the teaching and learning process.	There is limited evidence that the school leader attempts to develop partnerships between the school and the community, and only limited evidence that the school leader is aware of the benefits that this would bring to the process of teaching and learning.	There is clear evidence that the school leader establishes partnerships with some community groups that contribute to the success of the teaching and learning process.	There is clear, convincing, and consistent evidence that the school leader establishes solid, ongoing partnerships with a variety of community groups and organizations to strengthen school programs and support the success of the teaching and learning process.
An Involvement of all Stakeholders	There is little or no evidence that the school leader enlists the support of stakeholders in developing relationships with organizations outside the school to foster learning.	There is limited evidence that the school leader has enlisted the support of some stakeholders to develop relationships with organizations outside the school, but the purpose of these relationships may be unclear.	There is clear evidence that the school leader has enlisted the support of a variety of stakeholders to develop relationships with organizations outside the school, many of which are created to assist the school in fostering learning.	There is clear, convincing, and consistent evidence that the school leader has enlisted the support of a wide variety of stakeholders to develop relationships with organizations outside the school with the specific intent of assisting the school to foster learning.
A Demonstration of Ethical Behavior	There is little or no evidence that the school leader demonstrates fairness in engaging equal representation of the diverse school community in an attempt to foster learning.	There is limited evidence that the school leader demonstrates fairness in engaging some equal representation of the diverse school community in an attempt to foster learning.	There is clear evidence that the school leader frequently demonstrates equity and fairness in engaging representatives of the diverse school community in an attempt to foster learning.	There is clear, convincing, and consistent evidence that the school leader demonstrates equity and fairness in engaging representatives of the diverse school community in an ongoing basis to foster learning.

*These are the four central themes that unify the six Standards. They are fully described in Chapter 4 of this book.

Providing Opportunities for the Community and School to Serve Each Other

It is essential for the community to have meaningful involvement in the critical decisions that affect the quality of the schools' operations. The trust and commitment of the community to provide support and resources are dependent on their access and understanding of the vision and priorities for the improvement of the schools. As the official policy agent for the community, the Board of Education must have evidence of the summative and formative results of the schools' improvement objectives. The formal authority of the Board of Education is nourished by the community's perceptions of the efficiency of the schools.

The views of the community must be incorporated into the decision-making process in a timely manner and critical stakeholders must be identified. Viable vehicles must be identified for increased participation of the parents, community agencies, and taxpayers who have vested interest in the success of the schools. The realtors, senior citizens, and corporate and service agencies will make a determination of their confidence in the schools as a result of either their direct knowledge or the public relations and marketing efforts of the schools. Often public school educators take for granted their constituents and assume that the internal audience, i.e., faculty and staff, are most important.

The collaborations and formal and informal network of parents, teachers, and community agencies are essential for maintaining stability and continuity of values, aspirations, and expectations for the schools. We have the most valuable resource to the community, its youth and future taxpayers, who gain a sense of pride in the community through their service and reinforcement of the community norms and values.

Elaine Peeler Davis, Principal
Montclair High School
Montclair, New Jersey

Effective school leaders promote opportunities for the community and the school to serve each other within a symbiotic relationship. Each can serve and support the other, to the mutual advantage of both. Such a relationship depends on collaboration, communication, and trust. In this environment, both community and school can be open and ready to discuss specific ways in which each can help the other.

> "The views of the community must be incorporated into the decision-making process in a timely manner and critical stakeholders must be identified."

Both the community and the school have valuable resources. Some are unique to one or the other, but many can be reallocated for the mutual advantage of both. Resources that include facilities, expertise, services, and logistical support can often be shared and through the sharing made stronger and more valued. There are, of course, limits, and school and community leaders can work together to ascertain what those limits are, be they legal or logistical. By working together to determine how each can serve the other and how each must be independent, the school and the community can become stronger and be perceived by the public as acting responsibly. When all the resources of families, the community, and the school are appropriately brought to bear, students — the ultimate beneficiaries of such sharing — have a greater chance for success.

The truly effective school leader recognizes that, by establishing strong, ongoing, wide-ranging relationships with the community, members of the community become valuable resources in assisting the school in realizing its vision and supporting student learning in the classroom. Just as important, however, is this leader understanding that the school can be of assistance in bringing about improvements within the larger community. Developing effective, ongoing, reciprocal collaborations with the community is a sign of a perceptive, creative school leader. By integrating community-based initiatives within the existing curriculum, the leader can create deep and meaningful activities that will supplement classroom experiences and activities both in and outside the school building.

In establishing these community-based improvement efforts, the school leader makes use of the connections stakeholders have within the community. Stakeholders are used to generate ideas for how community members can support student learning in the classroom, and they can be used to identify many ongoing opportunities for the school to become active in community improvement efforts.

When engaging in these collaborative efforts within the community it is important that the school leader actively seeks participation from all representative groups within the school and community, that all stakeholders are treated equitably, and that all opinions are heard and valued. Furthermore, the school leader must be sure that these groups support each other's improvement efforts throughout the year, focusing always on the central goal of promoting the success of all students.

STANDARD 4: RELATIONSHIPS WITH THE BROADER COMMUNITY TO FOSTER LEARNING

A school administrator is an educational leader who promotes the success of all students by collaborating with families and community members, responding to diverse community interests and needs, and mobilizing community resources.

Component 4c: Providing Opportunities for the Community and School to Serve Each Other — Component Performance Table

LEVEL OF PERFORMANCE				
Central Themes *	**Rudimentary**	**Developing**	**Proficient**	**Accomplished**
A Vision for Success	There is little or no evidence that the school leader sees the school and community as anything other than separate and distinct entities or provides any opportunities for members of the community to engage in improvement efforts outside the school.	There is limited evidence that the school leader provides any opportunity for the school and community to engage in any meaningful way to achieve the school vision or provides any opportunities for the school community to engage in improvement efforts outside the school.	There is clear evidence that the school leader provides some opportunities for some community groups to serve the school in achieving its vision and clear evidence that the school leader encourages members of the school community to be active in supporting improvement efforts outside the school.	There is clear, convincing, and consistent evidence that the school leader provides a variety of opportunities for all appropriate community groups to address and help solve problems in a way that supports the school in achieving its vision, and that the leader ensures that members of the school community are active participants in improvement efforts.
A Focus on Teaching and Learning	There is little or no evidence that the school leader sees any potential benefit in developing partnerships or lines of communication with community youth and family service organizations to support the instructional program or provides any opportunities that might support community improvement.	There is limited evidence that the school leader uses community youth and service agencies to support the school program or has developed any opportunities for the instructional program to support community improvement.	There is clear evidence that the school leader integrates most community groups (e.g., youth and family service agencies, etc.) into many school programs that support and improve teaching and learning and has developed some instructional activities that support community improvement.	There is clear, convincing, and consistent evidence that the school leader fully integrates a variety of community groups (e.g., service agencies, cultural groups, etc.) in school programs to improve teaching and learning and that the school has instructional activities that support a variety of community improvement efforts throughout the year.
An Involvement of all Stakeholders	There is little or no evidence that the school leader involves stakeholders in developing ways that the school and the community might support each other's improvement efforts.	There is limited evidence that the school leader has enlisted the involvement of stakeholders to develop strategies that will provide members of the community an opportunity to foster learning in the school, and in finding ways for the school to assist the community in improvement efforts.	There is clear evidence that the school leader involves stakeholders in developing a variety of ways in which the community can assist the school to foster learning and for finding some opportunities for the school to help the community bring about improvement.	There is clear, convincing, and consistent evidence that the school leader continuously involves stakeholders in developing a comprehensive program to provide community members an opportunity to foster learning and to assist the school in becoming active in community improvement efforts.
A Demonstration of Ethical Behavior	There is little or no evidence that in activities in which the school and community serve each other, the school leader makes any attempt to seek participation from school and community members, is aware of equitable and respectful treatment of those involved, or is aware of appropriate ways the school and community could support each other.	There is limited evidence that in activities in which the school and community serve each other, the school leader seeks participation from representative groups within the school and community, treats stakeholders fairly, respects opinions, and works to ensure that the school and community support each other appropriately.	There is clear evidence that in most activities in which school and community serve each other, the school leader usually seeks participation from most representative groups within the school and community, treats all stakeholders fairly, respects all opinions, and works to ensure that the school and community support each other in an ethical manner.	There is clear, convincing, and consistent evidence that in all activities in which the school and community serve each other, the school leader actively seeks participation from all representative groups, treats all stakeholders equitably and respectfully, hears and values all opinions, and works to ensure that the school and community support each other in a fair and equitable manner.

*These are the four central themes that unify the six Standards. They are fully described in Chapter 4 of this bo

Understanding and Valuing Diversity

The American classroom and school is an increasingly multicultural landscape, and the school community is a microcosm of the world around us. The school leaders of tomorrow need to be familiar with the different cultural and ethnic groups that make up our school population and respect the many contributions each group makes to our school and school community. Perhaps the greatest evidence of our understanding and appreciation of diversity is in our daily work and our ability to engage students from every group in student activities and school success. School leaders need to invite, encourage, and engage representative members from our community to help in school improvement planning and in program development and review, and to have a voice and presence in their school.

Jack Walsh, Principal
Kodiak, Alaska

Effective school leaders understand and value the diversity of the school and the community and use their insights about diversity to foster learning. These leaders believe that in diversity lies strength and in unity lies strength. Effective school leaders understand and act on these seemingly disparate principles to promote the success of all students. They know that diversity can enrich the school community and through a shared appreciation of that diversity by the members of the school and community the strength of the school and the potential for success for all students can grow.

The school leader's relationship with and understanding of the community will provide the leader a deeper appreciation for the diversity that exists among the members of the community. Using this information, the school leader will ensure that the vision of the school reflects the community's diversity and that the vision will include high expectations for all students regardless of race/ethnicity, socioeconomic class, or gender. The effective leader also is sensitive to the subtle changes in teaching and learning that may result from this diversity and will make changes in the school program to ensure that these differences are accommodated. Furthermore, the school leader will support teachers in linking instruction to lessons that address cultural diversity and ensure that curriculum guides foster this instructional goal. In addition, this leader will provide multiple opportunities for the school and community to plan and participate in activities that celebrate the diversity of the community. Events that might recognize the diversity within the community and the world may include cultural programs (music, art, dance), small and large group school assembly programs featuring representatives of community groups that support this diversity, and other similar informative events. These programs are not "special events," but are ongoing throughout the year and form the very core of the social and cultural fabric of the school.

"... the school community is a microcosm of the world around us."

The effective school leader uses appropriate stakeholders to reach out to the diverse members of the community to ensure that each group is represented in decision-making activities in the school. The stakeholders also become useful in assisting the school leader to create a faculty and support staff that is representative of this diversity. This is accomplished by using these emissaries to create a network to support such activities as recruiting, interviewing, and hiring new faculty and staff that will more closely represent and reflect this diverse population.

The school leader must show respect for diversity and must model this attitude for the school community. Additionally, the leader must hold all the members of the school community accountable for this same value and must ensure that equity exists for students in all aspects of the school program.

Figure 6.16: Component 4d

STANDARD 4: RELATIONSHIPS WITH THE BROADER COMMUNITY TO FOSTER LEARNING

A school administrator is an educational leader who promotes the success of all students by collaborating with families and community members, responding to diverse community interests and needs, and mobilizing community resources.

Component 4d: Understanding and Valuing Diversity — Component Performance Table

	LEVEL OF PERFORMANCE			
Central Themes *	Rudimentary	Developing	Proficient	Accomplished
A Vision for Success	There is little or no evidence that the school leader has developed a vision for the school that is sensitive to the diversity within the community or sees the school as a microcosm of society.	There is limited evidence that the school leader attempts to create a school vision that includes success for all students and provides some limited means of acknowledging, in a positive way, the diversity of the community.	There is clear evidence that the school leader works for the creation of a school vision that includes high expectations for all students regardless of race, ethnicity, socioeconomic status, or gender, and provides opportunities for school and community to honor the diversity of the community.	There is clear, convincing, and consistent evidence that the school leader ensures the creation of a school vision that includes high expectations for all students regardless of race, ethnicity, socioeconomic status, or gender, and that the leader has provided multiple opportunities for the school and community to celebrate diversity.
A Focus on Teaching and Learning	There is little or no evidence that the school leader is either sensitive to or aware of diversity within the school community and the impact that this has on teaching and learning.	There is limited evidence that the school leader is sensitive to and aware of diversity within the school community, or ensures that the instructional program reflects the special needs that result from this diversity.	There is clear evidence that the school leader encourages teachers to plan and deliver differentiated lessons designed to address the needs of diversity within the community, that curriculum guides usually integrate cultural sensitivity and diversity, and that programs are developmentally appropriate for all students.	There is clear, convincing, and consistent evidence that the school leader has ensured that all teachers address cultural diversity, that students' differences are addressed in differentiated lesson plans, and that curriculum guides integrate cultural sensitivity and diversity in developmentally appropriate units of study.
An Involvement of all Stakeholders	There is little or no evidence that the school leader involves stakeholders to engage representatives of the diverse community in the decision-making process.	There is limited evidence that the school leader involves stakeholders to engage representatives of the diverse community in the decision-making process.	There is clear evidence that the school leader involves stakeholders in an attempt to engage representatives of the diverse community in many decision-making activities.	There is clear, convincing, and consistent evidence that the school leader involves appropriate stakeholders to ensure that representatives of the diverse community actively participate in decision-making.
A Demonstration of Ethical Behavior	There is little or no evidence that the school leader is sensitive to the issues of ethnicity, race, gender, and socioeconomic status among the students or larger community, or that the school leader treats others equitably.	There is limited evidence that the school leader respects the diversity within the school and community, expects others to do so, or addresses the need for equity in all aspects of the school program.	There is clear evidence that the school leader models respect for diversity within the school and community, usually holds members of the school community to that standard, and works to provide equity for students in all aspects of the school program.	There is clear, convincing, and consistent evidence that the school leader models respect for diversity within school and community, holds all members of the school community accountable for this value, and assures that equity exists for students in all aspects of the school program.

*These are the four central themes that unify the six Standards. They are fully described in Chapter 4 of this book.

A school administrator is an educational leader who promotes the success of all students by acting with integrity, with fairness, and in an ethical manner (CCSSO, 1996, p. 18).

STANDARD 5

The purpose of this Standard is to reflect the school leader's role in being the "first citizen" of the school or district community. School leaders set the tone for how employees and students will interact with each other and with other members of the school, district, and community. The school leader's dealings with students, parents, and employees must reflect concern for others as well as for the organization and the school leader's position. School leaders should develop an ability to examine personal and professional values as demonstrated through personal and professional codes of ethics. School leaders serve as role models, accepting responsibility and consequences for using their position constructively and productively for the school or district community. They work constructively with others in authority such as boards of education and other local and state policy-making bodies. In a culture of accountability, today's school leaders increasingly find themselves faced with an attempt to balance the total needs of children with public demands for increased student achievement. In resolving the dilemmas created by these sometimes-competing forces, the school leader must be guided by ethical principles. The school leader is an advocate for all children and their communities. The school leader champions the needs of students who face unique needs, such as language barriers, learning disabilities, socioeconomic disadvantages, and ethnic, racial, or lifestyle discrimination.

By honoring and championing the rights, needs, and contributions of all, by treating all stakeholders equitably and honestly, and by demonstrating a personal code of ethics at all times, the school leader does much to promote the success of all students (National Policy Board of Education Administration).

Each standard is framed by areas of focus defined by knowledge and skills, which may be evidenced at different levels of performance as indicated on the accompanying rubric tables. These areas of focus may be applied in different ways on the rubric tables. The leadership position (e.g., principal, superintendent, etc.) and context (e.g., elementary, secondary, urban, suburban, etc.) will determine their use.

STANDARD 5: INTEGRITY, FAIRNESS, AND ETHICS IN LEARNING

Areas of Focus	Knowledge and Skills
Integrity	▪ understands how one's office can be used in the service of all students and families to create a caring school community ▪ demonstrates honesty in all professional and personal endeavors and expects honesty in others
Fairness	▪ demonstrates impartiality when dealing with members of diverse groups ▪ exhibits sensitivity to the diversity within the school community
Ethics	▪ possesses a core set of values and beliefs that underlies the decision-making process that contributes to the common good

Demonstrating a Personal and Professional Code of Ethics

In my professional practice, demonstrating a personal and professional code of ethics has become my focus in the preparation of effective school leaders. I believe this is the foundation of leadership, the vehicle that drives all successful leaders. Our personal and professional code of ethics serves to guide our personal and professional behavior, and our interaction with others is usually governed by socially accepted rules. Leaders without a personal and professional code of ethics are often nomads in a desert of bad decisions. The impact on the school and community of leaders without a code of ethics can mean the success or failure of a school. Issues arise in schools today out of a variety of concerns. An overly narrow view tends to block reasoning and inquiry by excluding relevant and important human interests. Demonstrating a personal and professional code of ethics simply lets others know that you are concerned about how people are affected by the things that people do, and hence take another interest into account. By all means, effective leaders must have a vision, sustain a school culture and instructional program, demonstrate management and organizational skills, and have knowledge of the political, social, economic, legal, and cultural context of learning. However, a code of ethics has an impact on all aspects of your life and has direct results on whatever you do. Throughout my career, I have learned that if we are about the business of building effective schools and promoting student success, then effective educational leaders must act with integrity, fairness, and in an ethical manner.

Dr. Earl F. Newby
Eastern Kentucky University
Richmond, Kentucky

To be true leaders, school administrators must embody and demonstrate the deepest sense of personal and professional integrity, fairness, and ethics. Both in the community and in the school, these leaders must be honest and fair in their dealings with others and possess a set of personal standards grounded on a firm foundation of moral beliefs. This leadership must then translate these high principles into the operations of the school that support learning and promote the success of all students. This leadership is best demonstrated through the leader's creation of a vision for the school that is equitable for all the members of the school community, excludes no one from the opportunity to succeed, and actively assesses each person's progress toward the vision. One example of how this is accomplished is seen when the school leader assesses teacher and student performance on a continual basis, accurately represents the results of these assessments to the community, and confronts those who portray student achievement in a misleading way.

"Demonstrating a personal and professional code of ethics simply lets others know that you are concerned about how people are affected by the things that people do..."

The school leader must treat all the stakeholders in the school community in a consistently fair way and model this behavior to encourage this attitude in others. The leader must expect ethical behavior in all members of the school community and when unethical conduct is detected it must immediately be confronted and remedied by the leader.

To increase one's leadership capacity, the school leader must model ethical behavior in his or her personal activities outside, as well as in, the school. When an individual becomes a school leader, this person becomes a public figure as well. With leadership comes a mantle of responsibility that must be fulfilled for the school, for the sake of the students, and for the school community.

STANDARD 5: INTEGRITY, FAIRNESS, AND ETHICS IN LEARNING

A school administrator is an educational leader who promotes the success of all students by acting with integrity, with fairness, and in an ethical manner.

Component 5a: Demonstrating a Personal and Professional Code of Ethics — Component Performance Table

LEVEL OF PERFORMANCE			
Central Themes *	**Rudimentary**	**Developing**	**Proficient**	**Accomplished**
A Vision for Success	There is little or no evidence that the school leader has provided equitable opportunities for members of the school community to work toward the development and implementation of the school vision.	There is limited evidence that the school leader provides equitable opportunities for most members of the school community to work toward the development and implementation of the school vision, or has demonstrated integrity in ensuring each person's engagement in that pursuit.	There is clear evidence that the school leader fosters the development of a vision for success with concern that the vision addresses the needs of all students, actively promotes opportunities for each member of the school community to work toward the vision of the school, and fairly monitors each person's participation in that pursuit.	There is clear, consistent, and convincing evidence that the school leader ensures the development of a vision for success with equitable and ethical considerations for the needs of all students, applies the vision of the school equitably among all the members of the school community, excludes no one from the opportunity to succeed, and assesses each person's progress toward the vision.
A Focus on Teaching and Learning	There is little or no evidence that the school leader possesses a personal and professional code of ethics that is reflected in the behaviors and values of the staff and students in the teaching and learning process.	There is limited evidence that the school leader possesses a personal or professional code of ethics that is reflected in the behaviors and values of the staff and students in the teaching and learning process.	There is clear evidence that the school leader models personal and professional codes of ethics that are reflected in the behaviors and values of most of the staff and students in the teaching and learning process.	There is clear, consistent, and convincing evidence that the school leader models personal and professional codes of ethics that are clearly reflected in the behaviors and values of the staff and students in the teaching and learning process throughout the year.
An Involvement of all Stakeholders	There is little or no evidence that the school leader seeks to protect the stakeholders from the unethical behavior of others such as favoritism and exclusion of some groups from activities and opportunities.	There is limited evidence that the school leader treats stakeholders fairly, and opposes such inappropriate behavior as favoritism, withholding of information, or the exclusion of stakeholders from activities or opportunities.	There is clear evidence that the school leader treats members of the school community fairly, stands strongly against showing favoritism to or withholding information from any stakeholders or excludes any from activities or opportunities.	There is clear, consistent, and convincing evidence that the school leader consistently and genuinely treats all stakeholders fairly, vigorously expects ethical behavior in others, and is willing to confront those who fail to meet this expectation.
A Demonstration of Ethical Behavior	There is little or no evidence that the school leader is concerned about ethical behavior in the school or outside the school.	There is limited evidence that the school leader represents ethical behavior in the school or in personal activities outside the school.	There is clear evidence that the school leader demonstrates ethical behavior in the school and in personal activities outside the school.	There is clear, convincing, and consistent evidence that the school leader models ethical behavior both in the school and in personal activities outside the school.

*These are the four central themes that unify the six Standards. They are fully described in Chapter 4 of this boo

COMPONENT FIVE B

Understanding One's Impact on the School and Community

Perhaps the quality that most children, parents, and community members really expect from us is our personal commitment to the individual children we work with in our schools and our ability to remain objective, consistent, and fair. School community members measure this in the way we deal with situations and children on a daily basis, and there is a cumulative effect that shapes their general opinion of the school. For school leaders, this effect is complicated by our other roles as teacher, evaluator, teacher advocate, educational change agent, coach, and parent. The school leaders of tomorrow face an increasing expectation that decisions they make and policies they help set will remain above reproach and stand the most critical ethical tests. The faith of parents, students, and community members in the school leadership is the basis of their level of trust for the overall system and in turn their individual school. It is our personal integrity and ethical standards that help shape the tone and set the standard for all teachers and students in our school. School leaders cannot ignore the significance of the role they play in this overall picture.

Jack Walsh, Principal
Kodiak, Alaska

Effective school leaders understand that their behaviors, attitudes, actions, and decisions do have an impact on the school and the community-at-large. Seemingly insignificant decisions made by the school leader can seriously affect the climate of the school; just a callous comment to a parent can negatively impact the community. Effective leaders are sensitive to the influence they wield and realize that they must assess how the community reacts to this influence. Using surveys and other data collection devices frequently throughout the school year, the leader is able to monitor this reaction in the school and the community. Other ways leaders can feel the pulse of the community is by maintaining close ties with stakeholders in settings outside the school day. This is accomplished by attending community events, participating in local civic or religious organizations, or by frequently attending school cultural and athletic activities.

Simply gathering data is not enough, however. The leader must use the information obtained from these data collection efforts to gain an understanding of how his or her impact on the community will affect any attempt to achieve the vision of the school, the quality of the learning environment, and student achievement. Effective school leaders use this information to bring about positive change to the learning atmosphere and to promote the success of all students.

> *"The faith of parents, students, and community members in the school leadership is the basis of their level of trust for the overall system and in turn their individual school."*

The school leader frequently and regularly seeks assistance from members of the school and community to obtain feedback related to the administration's impact on learning. In addition, the leader seeks guidance and support from stakeholders to make appropriate use of this information to strengthen the relationship between the school and the community and to improve teaching and learning.

The effective school leader ensures that opportunities for discussions with stakeholders concerning the administration's impact on the school and the community are open and honest and carried out regularly throughout the school year. These dialogues are not simply scheduled for times that are politically expedient. Furthermore, the information gained from these conversations is used to support student learning, not to promote the political or personal agenda of any individual or group.

Figure 6.18: Component 5b

STANDARD 5: INTEGRITY, FAIRNESS, AND ETHICS IN LEARNING

A school administrator is an educational leader who promotes the success of all students by acting with integrity, with fairness, and in an ethical manner.

Component 5b: Understanding One's Impact on the School and Community —
Component Performance Table

	LEVEL OF PERFORMANCE			
Central Themes *	**Rudimentary**	**Developing**	**Proficient**	**Accomplished**
A Vision for Success	There is little or no evidence that the school leader has assessed the needs of the community or understands how the vision of the school affects these needs.	There is limited evidence that the school leader assesses the needs of the members of the community or the school, or uses any assessment information in any meaningful way to address these needs.	There is clear evidence that the school leader periodically assesses the needs of the members of the school and the community and considers this information to gain some understanding of how the vision of the school will affect these individuals in addressing their needs.	There is clear, convincing, and consistent evidence that the school leader continually assesses the needs of the members of the school and community on an ongoing basis and uses this information effectively to understand how the vision of the school will affect those individuals.
A Focus on Teaching and Learning	There is little or no evidence that the school leader seeks feedback from students and teachers to assess the administration's effect on the learning environment and student achievement.	There is limited evidence that the school leader seeks feedback from students and teachers to assess the administration's effect on the learning environment and student achievement, or that the school leader uses this information to consider how to improve the learning atmosphere.	There is clear evidence that the school leader seeks periodic feedback from students and teachers to assess the administration's effect on the learning environment and student achievement, and usually uses this information to consider positive change to the learning atmosphere.	There is clear, convincing, and consistent evidence that the school leader seeks frequent feedback from students and teachers to assess the administration's effect on the learning environment and student achievement, and consistently uses this information to bring about positive change to the learning atmosphere.
An Involvement of all Stakeholders	There is little or no evidence that the school leader seeks feedback from the members of the community about the administration's impact on learning.	There is limited evidence that the school leader seeks feedback from the members of the community about the administration's impact on learning or uses this information in a significant way.	There is clear evidence that the school leader periodically seeks some feedback from members of the community about the administration's impact on learning and uses this information in some ways to strengthen the relationship between the school and the community.	There is clear, convincing, and consistent evidence that the school leader frequently seeks feedback from the community about the administration's impact on learning and consistently uses this information to strengthen the relationship between school and community.
A Demonstration of Ethical Behavior	There is little or no evidence that the leader seeks input from or is concerned about the administration's impact on the school and community.	There is limited evidence that the school leader provides an opportunity for some members of the school community to provide information about the leader's impact on the school and community, and at times uses this information in making changes.	There is clear evidence that the school leader provides opportunities for an open and honest discussion with members of the school and community concerning the administration's impact and considers their opinions in making changes.	There is clear, convincing and consistent evidence that the school leader continuously provides opportunities for an open, honest, and constructive discussion with members of the school and community concerning the administration's impact and thoughtfully uses this information to bring about positive change.

*These are the four central themes that unify the six Standards. They are fully described in Chapter 4 of this book.

Respecting the Rights and Dignity of All

The principal has the responsibility to behave as a leader bonding the school community with shared values, ideas, and a commitment to keep the interests of the students to heart at all times. It is important to model your values, dreams, and hopes but also clearly and consistently to communicate them to the students, staff, and parents. In my 30 years as a principal, being sincere, honest, and respecting and accepting others has been a guide for me in the way I have organized my school and treated people. As the leader of the school community, I accept the responsibilities for my decisions to be fair and to be made wisely, and always to practice what I expect in others.

Margaret Pavol, Principal
Van Derveer School
Somerville, New Jersey

The effective school leader is sensitive to the rights of all stakeholders and acts to protect the personal dignity of all. Personal rights and freedoms of students, parents, and staff members must be protected and preserved in such a way that an environment conducive to learning is maintained. The effective leader knows that many decisions have to be made that satisfy both of these sometimes-competing demands. The leader keeps these principles in mind when attempting to ensure that the vision of the school is appropriate for all members of the school community, that all have an opportunity to attain the vision, and that all are supported in working toward the vision throughout the school year. To support this vision and to enhance teacher effectiveness, the school leader must ensure protection of the rights of teachers with respect to the fulfillment of their teaching duties. The school leader can help ensure the protection of these rights in many ways, for example:

■ By responding quickly and effectively to a teacher's personal or professional concern

■ By eliminating actions of outsiders that interfere with teaching and learning

■ By developing sound regulations and procedures that promote and protect an orderly climate for learning

> *"The principal has the responsibility to behave as a leader bonding the school community with shared values, ideas, and a commitment to keep the interests of the students to heart at all times."*

These activities help create an atmosphere conducive to learning and protect the teacher from distracting influences. Additionally, this teaching and learning environment is further enhanced when the leader ensures that no member of the school community places students or other individuals in embarrassing or humiliating situations. Young children and adolescents are particularly sensitive to any attention that singles them out for ridicule or that places them in awkward situations. The school leader must take steps to assure that the staff is cognizant of this and behaves in ways that protect the students and their egos.

The effective school leader promotes the rights and dignity of all by enlisting the support of all appropriate stakeholders. The efforts of the leader are magnified when appropriate members of the school community become engaged in developing activities that support the rights and dignity of all and then actually participate in these activities. One way the leader can use stakeholders in this enterprise is by involving them in efforts that develop stronger, ongoing relations with community agencies that support and guide children. The local police, bar association, or civic organizations are typically eager to come in to the school to assist in promoting the rights of all and to provide supplemental material for classroom instruction.

Finally, for the school leader to assure that the rights and dignity of all are protected, the leader creates and consistently supports rules and routines designed to accomplish this goal. These regulations are applied fairly and the leader actively confronts others who might seek to infringe on these rights.

STANDARD 5: INTEGRITY, FAIRNESS, AND ETHICS IN LEARNING

A school administrator is an educational leader who promotes the success of all students by acting with integrity, with fairness, and in an ethical manner.

Component 5c: Respecting the Rights and Dignity of All — Component Performance Table

	LEVEL OF PERFORMANCE			
Central Themes *	**Rudimentary**	**Developing**	**Proficient**	**Accomplished**
A Vision for Success	There is little or no evidence that the school leader has taken any measure to ensure that the vision of the school is appropriate for all members of the school community or that all have an opportunity to attain the vision.	There is limited evidence that the school leader has ensured either that the vision of the school is appropriate for all members of the school community or that all have an opportunity to attain the vision.	There is clear evidence that the school leader ensures that the vision of the school is appropriate for all members of the school community and all have an opportunity to attain the vision.	There is clear, convincing, and consistent evidence that the school leader ensures that the vision of the school is appropriate for all members of the school community, all have an opportunity to attain the vision, and all are supported in working toward the vision throughout the school year.
A Focus on Teaching and Learning	There is little or no evidence that the school leader is concerned with the rights and dignity of teachers or students.	There is limited evidence that the school leader demonstrates respect for the rights and dignity of teachers or students.	There is clear evidence that the school leader demonstrates respect for the rights and the dignity of all teachers and clearly advocates that the rights and dignity of all students are protected.	There is clear, convincing, and consistent evidence that the school leader demonstrates and insists on respect for the rights and dignity of all teachers and ensures that all students are treated with dignity and with full concern for their rights.
An Involvement of all Stakeholders	There is little or no evidence that the school leader is concerned with involving stakeholders in developing or participating in activities that support the rights and dignity of all.	There is limited evidence that the school leader provides opportunities for members of the school community to participate in or develop activities that support the rights and dignity of all.	There is clear evidence that the school leader provides some opportunities for members of the school community to participate in and/or develop activities that support the rights and dignity of all.	There is clear, convincing, and consistent evidence that the school leader provides frequent and various opportunities for all members of the school community to participate in and develop activities that support the rights and dignity of all throughout the school.
A Demonstration of Ethical Behavior	There is little or no evidence that the school leader is concerned with respecting or protecting the rights and dignity of teachers, students, or parents.	There is limited evidence that the school leader creates rules and routines that respect the rights of teachers, students, or parents, or enforces such rules or procedures effectively.	There is clear evidence that the school leader creates and routinely supports rules and routines that respect the rights of teachers, students, and parents.	There is clear, convincing, and consistent evidence that the school leader creates and consistently supports rules and routines that respect and protect the rights of teachers, students, and parents; and actively confronts efforts by others who might seek to infringe on these rights.

*These are the four central themes that unify the six Standards. They are fully described in Chapter 4 of this boo

Inspiring Integrity and Ethical Behavior in Others

In my professional experience, the ethical dilemmas have been numerous. I have been faced with complex questions that are not always easily answered. In the end, a decision had to be made that was fair and equitable to all. Determining what "equity" is and then making a decision that ensures a quality education for all children will push an educator to the limit. What is fair? Is it fair for more money to be spent on special education than on regular education? How do you fire a teacher who has been in the building for twenty years when no one has addressed the fact that the teacher is detrimental to children because of incompetence? These kinds of questions and many others face the educational leader of today. I found it encumbering but fulfilling to see the results of the decisions that were made that ultimately had a positive impact on the lives of children.

Rudy Duran, Ph.D.
Graduate School of Educational Leadership
University of Central Arkansas
Conway, Arkansas

The effective school leader takes responsibility for assuring that all members of the school community demonstrate integrity and behave in an ethical way in support of student learning. The leader of an educational institution must lead and motivate others to be ethical by example and by monitoring the actions of others with an ethical standard that is clear and made known to all. A leader must always be sure that the decisions he or she makes are always ethical and that unethical behavior of others will not be tolerated. A leader cannot inspire ethical behavior if he or she falls into the trap of "do as I say, not as I do." Having modeled ethical behavior, the leader is now in a position to be able to confront members of the school community who might have prevented others from working toward the vision of the school. The leader must not only confront these individuals but must take steps to successfully change their behavior. The leader must take these same steps in addressing issues that negatively impact the teaching and learning enterprise. The effective school leader will actively and continuously monitor school climate to assess the effects that the integrity and ethics of others have on the teaching and learning process. The leader must then act to remedy any barriers to learning that are identified.

"Determining what 'equity' is and then making a decision that ensures a quality education for all children will push an educator to the limit. "

In attempting to inspire integrity and ethical behavior in the school community, the effective school leader quickly learns that this cannot be done without help. The school leader can greatly broaden this effect among many more individuals by enlisting the support of all appropriate members of the community. Furthermore, this effect is magnified when the leader creates opportunities for these stakeholders to develop events designed specifically to recognize and reward those that demonstrate this attitude.

Finally, to inspire integrity and ethical behavior in others, the school leader must demonstrate these same traits. The truly effective leader is one who can show that his or her behavior specifically and directly caused others in the community to behave in the same way.

Figure 6.20: Component 5d

STANDARD 5: INTEGRITY, FAIRNESS, AND ETHICS IN LEARNING

A school administrator is an educational leader who promotes the success of all students by acting with integrity, with fairness, and in an ethical manner.

Component 5d: Inspiring Integrity and Ethical Behavior in Others — Component Performance Table

	LEVEL OF PERFORMANCE			
Central Themes *	**Rudimentary**	**Developing**	**Proficient**	**Accomplished**
A Vision for Success	There is little or no evidence that the school leader is aware of the need to create an environment in which all members of the school community act with integrity and a sense of ethics in any activities involving the school vision for success.	There is limited evidence that the school leader takes any actions designed to cause all members of the school community to act with integrity and a sense of ethics in working with the school vision for success.	There is clear evidence that the school leader works effectively with students, faculty, staff, and community to act with integrity and a sense of ethics as they create, implement, evaluate, and revise the school vision for success.	There is clear, convincing, and consistent evidence that the school leader is highly effective in inspiring students, faculty, staff, and community to demonstrate highest principles of integrity and ethical behavior as they create, implement, evaluate and revise the school vision for success.
A Focus on Teaching and Learning	There is little or no evidence that the school leader is aware of the impact that integrity and ethics have on the teaching and learning process.	There is limited evidence that the school leader is sensitive to the impact that integrity and ethics have on the teaching and learning process or is successful in addressing these types of issues as they arise.	There is clear evidence that the school leader is sensitive to the impact that integrity and ethics have on the teaching and learning process and demonstrates success in addressing these types of issues as they arise.	There is clear, convincing, and consistent evidence that the school leader actively and continuously monitors the school climate to assure that all aspects of the teaching and learning process are carried out with the highest regard for principles of integrity and ethical behavior.
An Involvement of all Stakeholders	There is little or no evidence that the school leader is aware of the value of enlisting the support of members of the community to inspire ethical behavior in others.	There is limited evidence that the school leader has enlisted the support of members of the community to inspire ethical behavior in others.	There is clear evidence that the school leader has enlisted the support of all appropriate stakeholders in creating an environment in which all behave with integrity and a sense of ethics.	There is clear, convincing, and consistent evidence that the school leader has enlisted the support of all appropriate stakeholders to model integrity and ethical behavior and to inspire these values in others and specifically recognizes and rewards their efforts.
A Demonstration of Ethical Behavior	There is little or no evidence that the school leader is aware of the responsibility to demonstrate ethical behavior as a model for other members of the school community.	There is limited evidence that the school leader behaves in a manner that would inspire a sense of integrity and ethical behavior in other members of the school community.	There is clear evidence that the school leader demonstrates a sense of integrity and ethical behavior that serves as a model for all members of the school community.	There is clear, convincing, and consistent evidence that the school leader consistently demonstrates a clear and compelling sense of integrity and ethical behavior that serves as a model for all members of the school community.

*These are the four central themes that unify the six Standards. They are fully described in Chapter 4 of this book.

A school administrator is an educational leader who has the knowledge and skills to promote the success of all students by understanding, responding to, and influencing the larger political, social, economic, legal, and cultural contexts (CCSSO, 1996, p. 20).

STANDARD

The success of students, and of the school in general, is greatly influenced by factors far removed from the school building, and,indeed, the school district. Political behavior of decision-makers outside the school, the social and economic composition of the district and state, legal considerations, and the very cultural make-up of the region all impinge on the school leader's attempt to provide educational opportunities of the highest quality for students. Sometimes these events and conditions promote learning, but at other times these factors might become barriers to student achievement. The purpose of this Standard is to make school leaders aware of these factors, understand why they exist, and find appropriate ways to respond to them. It is important that the school leader has the ability to develop a continuing dialogue with economic and political decision-makers concerning the vital role of schools and build collaborative relationships that support improved social and educational opportunities for children. Leaders must be prepared to participate actively in the political and policy-making context in the service of education, including proactive use of the legal system to protect student rights and improve student opportunities (National Policy Board of Education Administration).

Each Standard is framed by areas of focus defined by knowledge and skills, which may be evidenced at different levels of performance as indicated on the accompanying rubric tables. These areas of focus may be applied in different ways on the rubric tables. The leadership position (e.g., principal, superintendent, etc.) and context (e.g., elementary, secondary, urban, suburban, etc.) will determine their use.

STANDARD 6: THE POLITICAL, SOCIAL, ECONOMIC, LEGAL, AND CULTURAL CONTEXT OF LEARNING

Areas of Focus	Knowledge and Skills
Political	▪ knows the impact that political and policy-making decisions have on teaching and learning
Social	▪ knows how the social fabric of the larger community influences the educational enterprise
Economic	▪ understands the impact of economic conditions on the availability of resources and on teaching and learning
Legal	▪ understands the importance of operating the school within the law and how the law can be used to promote the success of all students
Cultural	▪ knows and understands the cultural context of the larger community and is able to use this knowledge to develop activities and policies that benefit students and their families

Operating Schools on Behalf of Students and Families

*It is my professional opinion, based on educational theory and professional
practice, that schools should exist to serve students and families. Schools
must develop a curriculum that addresses the academic and social needs of
the students. We can no longer afford to focus only on the students; we must
understand their family background. Schools, in order to ensure the success
of all students, must assist in the social, economic, and
moral support of the family.*

Dwight Luckett, Assistant Principal
Velma Jackson Magnet High School
Camden, Mississippi

One of the hallmarks of successful school leadership is the leader's ability to constantly focus on the fact that the school operates for the benefit of the students and their families. Schools were not created to provide employment for adult members of the community, nor were they created to provide a market for goods and services, although these might present positive side effects for the community. To ensure that schools do operate for students, the effective school leader must continuously assess the needs of the students and their families and use these data to create a vision for the school that promotes student success. In addition, this information informs the leader of the challenges faced by families within the community. Acquiring this knowledge base is critical if the leader is to understand and then address these issues as they impact the teaching and learning process.

The effective school leader collaborates with a variety of appropriate stakeholders throughout the school year to gain assistance in creating a school that is operated on behalf of the students and their families. The leader enlists the support of these stakeholders in assessing the needs of the students and families and in identifying and gathering resources necessary to address these needs in the classroom. These stakeholders might help the leader better understand these needs by placing the issues in a more relevant context and might then assist the leader in finding creative ways to secure the resources necessary to address these needs. Thus, stakeholders become critical allies of the school leader in establishing activities that identify barriers to learning and then in supporting teaching and learning to promote the success of all students.

Besides simply believing that the school operates on behalf of the students and their families, the effective school leader must ensure that all members of the school community share this same value. By constantly demonstrating this belief throughout the school year, the leader is able to begin to inspire this attitude among other members of the community.

"We can no longer afford to focus only on the students; we must understand their family backgrounds."

STANDARD 6: THE POLITICAL, SOCIAL, ECONOMIC, LEGAL, AND CULTURAL CONTEXT OF LEARNING

A school administrator is an educational leader who has the knowledge and skills to promote the success of all students by understanding, responding to, and influencing the larger political, social, economic, legal, and cultural contexts.

Component 6a: Operating Schools on Behalf of Students and Families — Component Performance Table

Central Themes *	LEVEL OF PERFORMANCE			
	Rudimentary	**Developing**	**Proficient**	**Accomplished**
A Vision for Success	There is little or no evidence that the school leader has any awareness of the need to consider the needs of students and families in the creation of the school vision.	There is limited evidence that the school leader considers the needs of students and parents in the creation of the school vision.	There is clear evidence that the school leader facilitates the creation of a school vision that is based on his or her understanding of the needs of the students and their families.	There is clear, convincing, and consistent evidence that the school leader considers a documented analysis of the needs of the community to facilitate the creation of a school vision based on the best interest of the students and their families.
A Focus on Teaching and Learning	There is little or no evidence that the school leader has any understanding of how teaching and learning are affected by issues faced by students and families outside the school.	There is limited evidence that the school leader is aware of the challenges faced by students and families within the community or understands how to address these issues as they impact teaching and learning.	There is clear evidence that the school leader is aware of the challenges faced by students and families within the community and has used this information in an attempt to improve teaching and learning.	There is clear, convincing, and consistent evidence that the school leader is aware of the challenges faced by students and families within the community and uses this information as part of an ongoing process to improve teaching and learning.
An Involvement of all Stakeholders	There is little or no evidence that the school leader is aware of the responsibility to collaborate with stakeholders to provide resources that support students and their families.	There is limited evidence that the school leader attempts to collaborate with stakeholders to provide resources that support students and their families.	There is clear evidence that the school leader collaborates with stakeholders to provide resources that support students and their families.	There is clear, convincing, and consistent evidence that the school leader is highly successful in collaborating with stakeholders throughout the year to provide resources that support students and their families.
A Demonstration of Ethical Behavior	There is little or no evidence that the school leader demonstrates integrity in ensuring that students and families are treated fairly, equitably, and with dignity.	There is limited evidence that the school leader demonstrates integrity in ensuring that some students and some families are treated fairly, equitably, and with dignity.	There is clear evidence that the school leader frequently demonstrates integrity in ensuring that most students and most families are treated fairly, equitably, and with dignity.	There is clear, convincing, and consistent evidence that throughout the school year, the school leader demonstrates integrity in ensuring that all students and families are treated fairly, equitably, and with dignity.

*These are the four central themes that unify the six Standards. They are fully described in Chapter 4 of this book.

Communicating Changes in Environment to Stakeholders

There is no doubt that the American public is beginning to desire choice in selecting schools for their children and demand accountability in learning. Both of these processes are irreversible trends. Some educators view these changes as the initial steps in the divesting of the monopoly of public education in America. Consequently, school-based administrators will need to become more adept in communicating changes in environment to stakeholders. In our preparation of principal candidates at Hood College, we constantly stress that schools will no longer be viewed as isolated islands in the sea of public education and that they must be leaders in explaining to stakeholders the environmental causal factors for required changes in the organization of learning for students.

Noel T. Farmer, Ed. D.
Associate Professor of Education
Hood College
Frederick, Maryland

Communicating changes in the environment to stakeholders is an often overlooked, but important, duty of the school leader. Frequently, changes in the community, the region, or the nation will have a direct impact on the local school. For instance, an announcement of the closing of a local industry that employs hundreds of community members will, most probably, have a sudden negative economic and emotional impact on the entire community and region. This event will have consequences for the students attending the local schools, their parents, and ultimately on the resources needed to support schools themselves. Conversely, an announcement of new employment opportunities coming into the community could have a positive impact on students, families, and the school. The school leader has an obligation to keep members of the school community aware of these changes in the environment and, more importantly, the impact that they will have on teaching and learning.

> *"...schools will no longer be viewed as isolated islands in the sea of public education..."*

Accomplished school leaders are those who possess a unique arsenal of skills and strategies that focus on promoting the success of all students. One of the biggest success factors possessed by those performing at this advanced level is the ability to anticipate change, understand how this change will impact the students and the teaching and learning process, and to take the steps necessary to meet the challenges presented by the change. High performing school leaders then anticipate changes in the environment and are ready to react to those changes. To accomplish this, the effective school leader establishes an ongoing dialogue with all members of the school and community to share information about these external forces. These leaders explain how these changes will impact the efforts of the school to work toward the school's vision and how these forces might challenge or support instructional programs and student achievement.

Not only does the effective school leader communicate this information to members of the school community and the community-at-large, but also the leader enlists the support of appropriate stakeholders in assuming some responsibility for this communication effort. The leader engages these stakeholders in creating opportunities for members of the community to enter into an ongoing dialogue about the issues and collaborates with the school on strategies that might be useful in confronting these external forces.

To ensure that his or her own professional ethics are not compromised, the effective school leader communicates changes in the environment throughout the year on an ongoing basis, and not just when it becomes a politically expedient way to leverage the self-interest of the leader or any special group. The leader also makes absolutely certain that this information is equally accessible to all the diverse members of the community.

Figure 6.22: Component 6b

STANDARD 6: THE POLITICAL, SOCIAL, ECONOMIC, LEGAL, AND CULTURAL CONTEXT OF LEARNING

A school administrator is an educational leader who has the knowledge and skills to promote the success of all students by understanding, responding to, and influencing the larger political, social, economic, legal, and cultural contexts.

Component 6b: Communicating Changes in Environment to Stakeholders — Component Performance Table

	LEVEL OF PERFORMANCE			
Central Themes *	**Rudimentary**	**Developing**	**Proficient**	**Accomplished**
A Vision for Success	There is little or no evidence that the school leader informs any members of the school or community about external forces that impact work toward the school's vision.	There is limited evidence that the school leader attempts to inform members of the school and/or community about some external forces that impact work toward the school's vision.	There is clear evidence that the school leader keeps members of the school and community informed about external forces that impact work toward the school's vision.	There is clear, convincing, and consistent evidence that the school leader maintains an ongoing dialogue with members of the school and community about external forces that impact work toward the school's vision.
A Focus on Teaching and Learning	There is little or no evidence that the school leader is aware of external forces that might challenge or support instructional programs and student achievement.	There is limited evidence that the school leader identifies external forces that might challenge or support instructional programs and student achievement, or communicates this information to the community when it is known.	There is clear evidence that the school leader identifies external forces that might challenge or support instructional programs and student achievement and communicates this information to the community.	There is clear, convincing, and consistent evidence that the school leader identifies external forces that might challenge or support instructional programs and student achievement, communicates this information to the community, and collaborates to assess the impact of these forces and plans accordingly.
An Involvement of all Stakeholders	There is little or no evidence that the school leader involves any stakeholder in communicating changes in the environment that might impact the operation of the school.	There is limited evidence that the school leader involves some stakeholders in communicating changes in the environment that might impact the operation of the school.	There is clear evidence that the school leader communicates with appropriate stakeholders about changes in the environment that might impact the operation of the school and about how school programs are impacted.	There is clear, convincing, and consistent evidence that the school leader continuously involves appropriate stakeholders in communicating any changes in the environment that might impact the operation of the school. In addition, the leader provides opportunities for members of the community to engage in a dialogue about these changes and adjust plans in light of them.
A Demonstration of Ethical Behavior	There is little or no evidence that the school leader communicates changes in the environment in an open, honest way that is accessible to all.	There is limited evidence that the school leader communicates changes in the environment in an open and honest way that is accessible to all the diverse community groups.	There is clear evidence that the school leader periodically communicates changes in the environment in an open and honest way that is accessible to all diverse community groups.	There is clear, convincing, and consistent evidence that the school leader communicates changes in the environment on an ongoing basis that is readily accessible to all diverse community groups in a manner that is honest, ethical, and unbiased.

*These are the four central themes that unify the six Standards. They are fully described in Chapter 4 of this book.

Working Within Policies, Laws, and Regulations

As a practicing principal and today as a practitioner preparer, I believe the cornerstone of our integrity rests in the ability to work within the framework of policies, laws, and regulations. The integrity I refer to is the ability to walk the walk, not just to talk the talk. If consistency of action is the goal, it is critical that we operate faithfully in accordance with Federal, state, local board, school building, and personal principles.

Dr. Jeanne Fiene
College of Education
Western Kentucky University
Bowling Green, Kentucky

Our nation's public schools operate under a comprehensive and complex set of local, state, and national policies, laws, and regulations. School leaders are mandated to work within each of these. Accomplished school leaders understand that there is no excuse for being ignorant of these laws and regulations that guide our schools or for simply ignoring them for the sake of expediency. Virtually all school-based laws and regulations have been enacted to protect members of the school community from harm, to ensure the mission of the school is carried out, and to protect the public's investment in the educational process. Flaunting these regulations can have disastrous consequences for the school leader, and, in many cases, the entire school community. While all school leaders must be knowledgeable about the legalities that govern the operation of the school, the effective leader understands how to use this knowledge to further promote, support, and enhance the vision of the school. Likewise, this leader has an understanding of how these laws and policies can actually bring about significant, positive change in teaching and learning that impacts all student groups.

The effective school leader also is aware of, and sensitive to, the policies, laws, and regulations that govern how the school may collaborate with stakeholders and ensures that all stakeholders operate only within the limits of those regulations. One of the more obvious examples here is that of pupil confidentiality. Federal, state, and local laws are very precise in identifying who may have access to pupil records and for what purpose. While it is extremely beneficial to engage appropriate stakeholders in school activities, the wise leader must use caution in protecting the rights of students, teachers, and staff.

The ethical school leader abides by the spirit as well as the intent of policies, laws, and regulations that govern the school and society throughout the year. The leader understands what these regulations are designed to accomplish and is meticulous in adhering to these principles. Furthermore, this leader's behavior is demonstrated both in the school and in the larger community. Finally, this leader assumes full responsibility for attempting to inspire others to that same behavior.

"...the cornerstone of our integrity rests in the ability to work within the framework of policies, laws, and regulations."

STANDARD 6: THE POLITICAL, SOCIAL, ECONOMIC, LEGAL, AND CULTURAL CONTEXT OF LEARNING

A school administrator is an educational leader who has the knowledge and skills to promote the success of all students by understanding, responding to, and influencing the larger political, social, economic, legal, and cultural contexts.

Component 6c: Working Within Policies, Laws, and Regulations — Component Performance Table

| Central Themes * | LEVEL OF PERFORMANCE | | | |
	Rudimentary	Developing	Proficient	Accomplished
A Vision for Success	There is little or no evidence that the school leader considers any policies, laws, or regulations that govern the operation of the school to support the vision of the school.	There is limited evidence that the school leader is familiar with the policies, laws, and regulations that govern the operation of the school, or uses this information to support the vision of the school.	There is clear evidence that the school leader is aware of the policies, laws, and regulations that govern the operation of the school and takes appropriate measures to be sure the school adheres to these governances to support the vision of the school.	There is clear, convincing, and consistent evidence that the school leader is highly knowledgeable about the policies, laws, and regulations that govern the operation of the school and uses this knowledge to further promote, support, and enhance the vision of the school.
A Focus on Teaching and Learning	There is little or no evidence that the school leader uses knowledge of policies, laws, or regulations that govern the school to bring about any positive change in teaching and learning.	There is limited evidence that the school leader has an understanding of how policies, laws, and regulations that govern the school can be used to bring about positive change in teaching and learning.	There is clear evidence that the school leader is aware of policies, laws, and regulations that govern the school and has used this information to bring about some positive change in teaching and learning.	There is clear, convincing, and consistent evidence that the school leader is knowledgeable about the policies, laws, and regulations that govern the school and uses this knowledge to bring about significant, positive change in teaching and learning that impacts all student groups.
An Involvement of all Stakeholders	There is little or no evidence that the school leader collaborates with stakeholders within the structure of the policies, laws, and regulations that govern the school, or ensures that stakeholders operate only within the limits of those regulations.	There is limited evidence that the school leader collaborates with stakeholders within the structure of the policies, laws, and regulations that govern the school and ensures that stakeholders operate only within the limits of those regulations.	There is clear evidence that the school leader collaborates with appropriate stakeholders within the structure of the policies, laws, and regulations that govern the school and attempts to ensure that all stakeholders operate only within the limits of those regulations.	There is clear, convincing, and consistent evidence that the school leader collaborates with appropriate stakeholders within the structure of the policies, laws, and regulations that govern the school and ensures that all stakeholders operate only within the limits of those regulations.
A Demonstration of Ethical Behavior	There is little or no evidence that the school leader abides by the spirit or the intent of policies, laws, and regulations that govern the school and society.	There is limited evidence that the school leader abides by the spirit, as well as the intent, of policies, laws, and regulations that govern the school and society.	There is clear evidence that the school leader abides by the spirit, as well as the intent, of policies, laws, and regulations that govern the school and society.	There is clear, convincing, and consistent evidence that, throughout the year, the school leader abides by the spirit, as well as the intent, of policies, laws, and regulations that govern the school and society, and inspires others to that same behavior.

*These are the four central themes that unify the six Standards. They are fully described in Chapter 4 of this book.

COMPONENT SIX D

Communicating With Decision-Makers
Outside the School Community

Many administrators do not recognize the influence they have on state and federal decision-makers regarding legislative issues that affect education. I belong to my state and national principal's association that hires people to lobby for legislation that is in the best interest of kids. I support a coalition that financially supports political candidates who have earned a positive track record for education. I subscribe to the coalition's legislative newsletter and contact my representatives on legislative issues. Administrators must play an active role in the political arena to assure the success for all students.

Mrs. Dolores Stegner, Principal
David Barton Elementary
Boonville, Missouri

Establishing lines of communication with decision-makers outside the school community is critically important in successful school leadership. These individuals from outside the school, whether political figures, agents of a state department of education, or members of some other influential group, continually create policies and regulations that impact the school. Their influence may be economical, financial, educational, or significant in one of many other meaningful ways. Still other groups, although not technically decision-makers, influence the school in other ways. These might include the local Chamber of Commerce and similar business-related organizations, actual local businesses, colleges and universities, religious groups, the media, and other centers of influence. The effective school leader understands the importance of establishing positive relationships with these groups and individuals and understands how to use these relationships to build a dialogue with the decision-makers. Through this ongoing dialogue, the leader will have the ability to make outside decision-makers aware of the vision of the school and how they can support and shape it. In addition, the leader can help these individuals understand and appreciate the efforts of teachers and students and how these decision-makers can effectively influence and improve student performance and instruction.

To build and sustain the communication system with outside decision-makers, the effective school leader collaborates with appropriate stakeholders to form networks. These networks are designed to facilitate effective communication with these decision-makers and to broaden the scope of those included in this communication effort.

"Administrators must play an active role in the political arena to assure the success for all students."

Finally, the effective school leader understands the importance of enlisting outside decision-makers to support the success of all students. The leader ensures that all students receive equal benefit from those outside the school. At the same time, the leader is aware of, and concerned with, the ethical motivations of these decision-makers and how these motivations might impact the school climate or the school's relationship with the larger community.

Figure 6.24: Component 6d

STANDARD 6: THE POLITICAL, SOCIAL, ECONOMIC, LEGAL, AND CULTURAL CONTEXT OF LEARNING

A school administrator is an educational leader who has the knowledge and skills to promote the success of all students by understanding, responding to, and influencing the larger political, social, economic, legal, and cultural contexts.

Component 6d: Communicating with Decision-Makers Outside the School Community — Component Performance Table

| Central Themes * | LEVEL OF PERFORMANCE | | | |
	Rudimentary	Developing	Proficient	Accomplished
A Vision for Success	There is little or no evidence that the school leader makes any efforts to make decision-makers outside the school aware of the vision of the school.	There is limited evidence that the school leader makes decision-makers outside the school aware of the vision of the school.	There is clear evidence that the school leader has established a dialogue with decision-makers outside the school and makes them aware of the vision of the school.	There is clear, convincing, and consistent evidence that the school leader has established an ongoing dialogue with decision-makers outside the school, shares with them the vision of the school and how they can support and shape it.
A Focus on Teaching and Learning	There is little or no evidence that the school leader makes any attempt to communicate with decision-makers outside the school concerning the efforts of teachers and students.	There is limited evidence that the school leader provides information to decision-makers outside the school concerning the efforts of teachers and students.	There is clear evidence that the school leader has provided information to decision-makers outside the school concerning the efforts of teachers and students and discusses with these decision-makers how they can influence and improve instruction and student performance.	There is clear, convincing, and consistent evidence that the school leader has established an ongoing dialogue with decision-makers outside the school concerning the efforts of teachers and students and how these decision-makers can effectively influence and improve instruction and student performance.
An Involvement of all Stakeholders	There is little or no evidence that the school leader makes any attempts to collaborate with any stakeholder to form networks with decision-makers outside the school.	There is limited evidence that the school leader collaborates with stakeholders in an attempt to form networks with decision-makers outside the school.	There is clear evidence that the school leader collaborates with appropriate stakeholders to form networks with decision-makers outside the school for the improvement and support of teaching and learning.	There is clear, convincing, and consistent evidence that the school leader collaborates throughout the school year with appropriate stakeholders, forming networks designed to facilitate effective communication with decision-makers outside the school for the improvement and support of teaching and learning.
A Demonstration of Ethical Behavior	There is little or no evidence that the school leader's communications with decision-makers outside the school is open or honest.	There is limited evidence that the school leader's communications with decision-makers outside the school is open or honest.	There is clear evidence that the school leader communicates openly and honestly with decision-makers outside the school in support of the success of all students.	There is clear, convincing, and consistent evidence that the school leader communicates openly and honestly with decision-makers outside the school in support of the success of all students. Further, the school leader provides these decision-makers guidance in understanding the purpose of education and how their actions impact the school.

*These are the four central themes that unify the six Standards. They are fully described in Chapter 4 of this book.

CHAPTER 7

CONCLUSION: THE CHALLENGES OF IMPLEMENTING THE FRAMEWORK

The challenge now before us is to take this framework for school leaders and use it to promote the professional growth of our school leaders and to shape public opinion about the very nature of effective school leadership.

> For each of these standards (ISLLC Standards for School Leaders), administrators must develop a deep understanding of what must be improved and skill in how to do it; must believe in, value, and be committed to their importance and implications; and must facilitate processes and engage in activities to ensure that the goals are met. Many more leaders will become effective if these skills and knowledge are explicitly taught. To meet these worthy goals for what school leaders should know and do, society must provide them with better professional development (National Staff Development Council, December 2000. P. 4).

The framework presented in this book, designed to cultivate and enhance the professional behavior and skills of school leaders is, of course, based on the *ISLLC Standards for School Leaders*. The ISLLC Standards started to bring about significant changes in the quality and reaffirmation of the role of school leaders long before we ever thought of creating the framework for school leaders. Chief among these changes are new ways of assessing the knowledge, skills, and abilities of potential school leaders; implementation of new framework-based programs; new ways to think about resource allocation related to reform efforts; and new ways to train, select, nurture, and support school leaders.

Standards-based Assessment

Many of these changes were precipitated as a result of the development and administration of a series of tests used by states as part of their licensing requirements for aspiring school principals, superintendents, and other school leaders. Educational Testing Service developed this series, known as the School Leadership Series (SLS) of licensure assessment, under contract with the Interstate School Leaders Licensure Consortium (ISLLC) and the Council of Chief State School Officers (CCSSO). The School Leadership Series consists of three licensure assessments that measure the ability of candidates to demonstrate their awareness of the ISLLC Standards and their ability to apply these Standards to real-life situations presented as case studies, shorter vignettes, or through a portfolio assessment. The introduction of these standards-based assessments has reinforced an appreciation among decision-makers of the role of the principal and superintendent that centers on teaching and learning, and promoting the success of all students.

Implementing Framework-based Programs

Decision-makers will be required to address some challenges in implementing a framework-based program for the improvement and support of school leaders. Some of these issues include reliability of the program and a reallocation of resources.

Reliability is a measure of the confidence in the result shown by an assessment or activity. Reliability is a critical measure in any high-stakes assessment (e.g., pass or fail judgments for licensure), or for accountability, as in confirming the success of new curricula, or an instructional or professional training program. The reliability of the evaluation of a framework-based program can be enhanced by:

- *Standardizing* the implementation and rating processes used for evaluation

- *Training* those responsible for implementing and evaluating all the aspects of the framework-based program

The second challenge of implementing framework-based programs will involve the expenditure of existing or new resources. However,

> Improving the quality of America's school leaders is the most feasible way to make a significant difference in American education. Beyond the fact that improving principal performance produces great leverage over school achievement at limited cost, school systems owe it to their communities to ensure that all principals meet high standards of performance and they are engaged in sustained, serious study of the most effective ways to improve student learning. (National Staff Development Council, December 2000. P.15).

These resources of costs are finite and consist of things beyond money, such as personnel, time, and facilities, among other considerations. Furthermore, there will be many competing claims for these limited assets. For instance, one form of a competing claim might be lost opportunity costs (e.g., if we use this money to train school leaders we cannot use it to buy basketballs).

To reallocate resources appropriately, decision-makers will be required to make a significant paradigm shift in thinking about leadership and school leaders. Part of this new thinking will include such considerations as the following:

- Realizing that the *responsibility* of the leader is now defined in terms of the Standards, "promoting the success of all students"

- Realizing that the same *expectations* for learning and accountability that they expect of students and faculty must be extended to the school leader

- Realizing that these responsibilities and expectations must be *supported and rewarded*

Once the shift in the view of leadership is made, the school community must be willing to channel resources to fund that investment. Facilitated by the school leader, stakeholders must begin to think about allocating assets in new ways by:

- *Establishing priorities* for leader training and assessment

- *Conducting a district inventory* of existing training opportunities and performance assessment instruments for school leaders and ensuring that these are adequate to meet the needs of the district and its leaders

- *Reallocating resources* to meet the mission and vision of the school and district

- *Exploring creative ways* to generate additional resources

Conclusion

Richard Elmore (2000), a professor at the Graduate School of Education at Harvard, has stated,

> Leaders must lead by modeling the values and behaviors that represent collective good. Role-based theories of leadership wrongly envision leaders who are empowered to ask of or require others to do things they may not be willing or able to do. But if learning, individual and collective, is the central responsibility of leaders, then they must be able to model that which they expect or require others to do. Likewise, leaders should expect to have their own practice subjected to the same scrutiny as they exercise toward others (p. 21).

It has been posited that some school leaders are reluctant to participate in professional development programs because the school community might view their involvement as a sign of inadequate preparation or as evidence of their inability to lead. After all, one might challenge, "Why were you selected principal if you still need training?" What many fail to recognize, however, is that the most accomplished professional golfer still spends hours at the practice tee before and after each tournament. And as professionals, school leaders must model life-long learning and join their communities of learners.

The educational future of our children and of our schools demands that we, collectively, begin to look for new and better ways to train, select, nurture, and support our current and new school leaders. The *ISLLC Standards for School Leaders* gives us an excellent place to start. These Standards help us define the role of the leader and the knowledge and skills required of our leaders. University programs that prepare aspiring school leaders in the states that have adopted ISLLC standards-based assessments, as well as universities in many other states, have already begun to alter the way these aspiring leaders are trained and now include standards-relevant material in the curriculum (see Chapter 2).

Exciting and challenging changes in the landscape of school leadership are at hand. Imperatives for new standards-based assessments and programs, new ways to allocate resources, and new visions for professional development all figure prominently in that landscape. In the quest for professionally powerful ways to bring about these changes, when used responsibly, the framework and the ISLLC Standards, it is hoped, will be an important means for promoting and sustaining a new vision of leadership.

Used constructively and thoughtfully, the framework can serve to remind us of our commitment to our children, and to serve as a kind of roadmap to help us find our way through that new landscape of school leadership. We take the journey for our students, all our students. Despite the roadblocks and potholes and stop signs, taking the journey is a noble effort.

APPENDIX

A PARTIAL LIST OF THE RESEARCH USED IN THE DEVELOPMENT OF THE ISLLC STANDARDS

The ISLLC Standards for School Leaders are scaffolded on the knowledge base that connects the work of school leaders (principals, superintendents, and others) to more effective organizational performance, especially student learning outcomes. That empirical knowledge base is laid out in the following writings of the Chair of ISLLC, all of which pre-date the release of the Standards. Readers who desire more detailed information on the studies that support the Standards are directed to the references in the articles, chapters, and books listed in Appendix A. Furthermore, recent empirical work in support of the Standards can be reviewed in: Murphy, et al (2001). *The Productive High School.* Newbury Park, CA: Corwin Press.

Beck, L. G., & Murphy, J. (1996). *The Four Imperatives of a Successful School.* Newbury Park, CA: Corwin/Sage.

Murphy, J. (1994, December). The changing role of the superintendency in restructuring districts in Kentucky. *School Effectiveness and School Improvement,* 5(4), 349-375.

Murphy, J. (1994). Transformational change and the evolving role of the principalship: Early empirical evidence. In J. Murphy & K. S. Louis (Eds.), *Reshaping the Principalship: Insights from Transformational Reform Efforts.* Newbury Park, CA: Corwin Press.

Murphy, J., & Hallinger, P. (1993).Restructuring schooling: Learning from ongoing efforts. In J . Murphy & P. Hallinger (Eds.), *Restructuring schooling: Learning from ongoing efforts.* Newbury Park, CA: Corwin Press.

Leithwood, K., Hallinger, P., & Murphy, J. (1993). The expertise of educational leaders. In P. Hallinger, K. Leithwood, & J. Murphy (Eds.), *Cognitive Perspectives on Educational Leadership.* New York: Teachers College Press.

Murphy, J. (1993, May). Restructuring schooling: The equity infrastructure. *School Effectiveness and School Improvement,* 4(2), 111-130.

Murphy, J. (1992). School effectiveness and school restructuring: Contributions to educational improvement. *School Effectiveness and School Improvement,* 3(2), 90-109.

Murphy, J. (1992). *The Landscape of Leadership Preparation: Reframing the Education of School Administrators.* Newbury Park, CA: Corwin/Sage.

Evertson, C., & Murphy, J. (1992). Beginning with classrooms: Implications for restructuring schools. In H. H. Marshall (Ed.), *Redefining Student Learning.* Norwood, NJ: Ablex.

Murphy, J. (1990). The educational reform movement of the 1980s: A comprehensive analysis. In J. Murphy (Ed.), *The Reform of American Public Education in the1980s: Perspectives and Cases.* Berkeley, CA: McCutchan.

Murphy, J. (1990). Management of effective schools. In T. Husen and T. N. Postlethwaite (Eds.), *International Encyclopedia of Education: Research and Studies, Supplementary,* (Vol. 2).

Murphy, J. (1990). Principal instructional leadership. In L. S. Lotto & P. W. Thurston (Eds.), *Advances in Educational Administration: Changing Perspectives on the School.* (Volume 1, Part B). Greenwich, CT: JAI Press.

Murphy, J. (1989, Fall). Educational reform in the 1980s: Explaining some surprising success. *Educational Evaluation and Policy Analysis,* 11, (3), 209-223.

Murphy, J., & Hallinger, P. (1989, March-April). Equity as access to learning: Curricular and instructional treatment differences. *Journal of Curriculum Studies,* 21(2), 129-149.

Murphy, J., & Hallinger, P. (1988, February). The characteristics of instructionally effective school districts. *Journal of Educational Research,* 81(3), 175-181.Reprinted in *Outcomes,* Winter 1990, 8(4), 26-33.

Murphy, J., Hull, T., & Walker, A. (1987, July-August). Academic drift and curricular debris: Analysis of high school course-taking patterns with implications for local policy makers. *Journal of Curriculum Studies,* 19(4), 341-360.

Murphy, J., & Hallinger, P. (1986, Summer). The superintendent as instructional leader: Findings from effective school districts. *Journal of Educational Administration,* 24(2), 213-236.

Hallinger, P., & Murphy, J. (1986, May). The social context of effective schools. *American Journal of Education,* 94 (3), 328-355. Reprinted in *Educational Excellence Network,* 6, 9-22.

Hallinger, P., & Murphy, J. (1985, November). Assessing the instructional management behavior of principals. *Elementary School Journal,* 86(2), 217-247.

Murphy, J., Weil, M., Hallinger, P., & Mitman, A. (1985, Spring). School effectiveness: A conceptual framework. *The Educational Forum,* 49(3), 361-374.

Murphy, J., Mesa, R. P., & Hallinger, P. (1984, July). Creating effective school districts: Lessons from practice, research, and national reports. *American Education,* 20(6), 13-14.

APPENDIX B

THE PROFESSION OF SCHOOL ADMINISTRATOR: AN ANALYSIS OF THE RESPONSIBILITIES AND KNOWLEDGE AREAS IMPORTANT FOR BEGINNING SCHOOL ADMINISTRATORS (Tannenbaum, 1999)

(A SUMMARY OF FINDINGS)

ABSTRACT

The Interstate School Leaders Licensure Consortium (ISLLC) of the Council of Chief State School Officers is sponsoring the development of a performance-based licensure assessment of beginning school principals. Educational Testing Service (ETS) has been contracted to develop the assessment and scoring systems. The development effort is guided by two sources of information, the ISLLC Standards for School Leaders and a national job analysis study. This report describes the job analysis study conducted by ETS. The purpose of this study was to identify responsibilities and knowledge areas important for beginning school principals. Job experts defined a domain consisting of 103 responsibility statements and 98 knowledge statements. A national survey of 2,460 elementary, middle, and secondary school principals confirmed the importance of the domain. An aggregate analysis indicated that all 103 responsibility statements (a mean ≥ 3.50). All but 2 of the 98 knowledge statements were judged to be important. Subgroup analysis identified three responsibility statements and three knowledge statements that did not meet the cutoff value of 3.50. In total, 100 of 103 responsibility statements (97%) and 93 of 98 knowledge statements (95%) were judged to be important.

Rank Order of Importance: Dimensions of the Job Domain for the Position of School Administrator

RANK ORDER	CATEGORY
1st	Leadership
2nd	Strategic Planning
3rd	Facilitating Student Learning
4th	Developing, Implementing, and Evaluating Curriculum and Instruction Selecting
5th	Supervising and Evaluating Faculty and Support Staff
6th	Relations with Faculty and Support Staff
7th	Professional Development
8th	Community Relations
9th	Management
10th	Maintaining the Physical Security of Students, Faculty, and Support Staff
11th	Operations

TABLE 5. LINKAGES BETWEEN THE ISLLC STANDARDS AND JOB ANALYSIS CATEGORIES

Job Analysis Categories (Responsibilities and knowledge)	ISLLC STANDARDS					
	1	2	3	4	5	6
Leadership	4k, 5k, 6k	9k, 18p	7k, 3p, 7p,15p,16p, 17p, 18p	1k	4k, 1p, 2p	4k
Strategic Planning	2k, 4k, 1p 4p, 9p, 10p 12p, 15p		4k, 4p, 23p		6p	
Facilitating Student Learning		1k, 2k, 7k 10k, 1p, 3p 9p, 10p, 16p 19p		3k, 14p	8p, 9p	8k
Developing, Implementing & Evaluating Curriculum & Instruction		5k, 6k, 10k 12p, 13p 16p	7k, 13p			3k
Selecting, Supervising, & Evaluating Faculty & Support Staff		5k, 6k, 9p	4k, 7k, 22p		15p	3k
Relationships with Faculty & Support Staff		3k, 8k, 1p 3p	16p, 17p, 18p		3k, 8p, 9p, 10p	
Professional Development		6k, 8k, 10k, 2p, 7p, 9p	4k, 10p, 22p		4p	
Community Relations	5k, 1p, 7p			3k, 4k, 5k, 1p, 2p, 3p, 4p, 6p, 7p, 8p, 12p, 13p,15p	10p	8k, 2p, 3p
Management	4k, 11p, 13p		2k, 5k, 7k, 2p, 4p, 5p, 7p, 9p, 15p 20p, 23p		15p	3k
Maintaining the Physical Security of Student, Faculty, & Support Staff			3k, 7k, 6p 21p 2k, 5k, 7k, 8k, 2p, 4p, 6p, 20p, 21p			3k

NOTE: **k** refers to **knowledge** indicator, **p** refers to **performance** indicator, and the number preceding each **k** or **p** represents the number of the indicator. There are no **disposition** indicators because the assessment is not designed to address dispositions.

Each ISLLC Standard was linked to three or more of the 11 job categories; and in most cases, the linkages were secured by connections to multiple performance indicators or multiple knowledge indicators. This network of linkages supports the functional relationship between the job analysis categories and the ISLLC Standards.

THE PROFESSION OF SCHOOL SUPERINTENDENT: AN ANALYSIS OF THE RESPONSIBILITIES AND KNOWLEDGE AREAS IMPORTANT FOR BEGINNING SCHOOL SUPERINTENDENTS (Latham and Holloway, 1999)

(A SUMMARY OF FINDINGS)

ABSTRACT

The Interstate School Leaders Licensure Consortium (ISLLC) of the Council of Chief State School Officers is sponsoring the development of a performance-based licensure assessment of beginning school superintendents. Educational Testing Service (ETS) has been contracted to develop the assessment and scoring systems. The development effort is guided by two sources of information, the ISLLC Standards for School Leaders and a job analysis study conducted in Missouri and North Carolina. This report describes the job analysis study conducted by ETS. The purpose of this study was to identify responsibilities and knowledge areas important for beginning school superintendents. Job experts defined a domain consisting of 124 responsibility statements and 123 knowledge statements. Surveys were mailed to all superintendents in Missouri and North Carolina. Approximately 50% of superintendents (n=318) responded, and confirmed the importance of the domain. An aggregate analysis indicated that all of the 124 responsibility statements (100%) were judged to be important, and all but four of the 123 knowledge statements (96.75%) were judged to be important. Subgroup analysis identified all but one of the 124 responsibility statements (99.2%) as judged to be important and all but twelve of the 123 knowledge statements (90.2%) as judged to be important.

RANK ORDER OF IMPORTANCE: DIMENSIONS OF THE JOB DOMAIN FOR THE POSITION OF SUPERINTENDENT OF SCHOOLS

RANK ORDER	CATEGORY
1st	School Board Relations
2nd	Developing and Maintaining an Effective School and District Staff
3rd	Facilitating Student Learning
4th	Community Involvement and Collaboration
5th	Organizational Resources and Operations
6th	Developing, Implementing, and Evaluating Curriculum/Instruction
7th	Professional Development for School and District Staff
8th	Group Processes
9th	Understanding and Responding to the Larger Political Context

TABLE 4. LINKAGES BETWEEN THE ISLLC STANDARDS AND JOB ANALYSIS CATEGORIES

Job Analysis Categories (Responsibilities and knowledge)	ISLLC STANDARDS					
	1	2	3	4	5	6
Group Processes	K(1, 2, 4, 5, 6,) P(1–4, 6–11, 13, 14, 15)	K(3, 6, 7 ,9) P(1, 3, 8, 13, 14, 16, 18)	K(4, 5) P(2, 3, 4, 7–10, 13–18, 22)	K(1) P(11, 15, 16)	P(1–4, 6, 8)	P(4)
Facilitating Student Learning	K(1, 4–6) P(1, 2, 5, 6, 8, 10, 12)	K(1–7, 9–11) P(1–6, 8–20)	P(2, 3, 4, 18, 19, 21, 22)	K(1, 2, 3) P(1, 2, 4, 6-9, 11, 13)	K(2–5) P(7–10, 12,16)	K(4, 5)
Developing, Implementing & Evaluating Curriculum & Instruction	K(1, 2, 4) P(10)	K(2, 4–6, 10) P(9, 12–19)	K(1, 7) P(1, 3)		P(15, 16)	K(3, 7) P(4)
Developing and Maintaining an Effective School and District Staff	K(2, 5, 6) P(2, 4 ,5, 7 ,9, 12, 13, 14)	K(3, 5, 7, 8) P(1–4, 8, 10, 12, 15, 16, 19, 20)	K(1, 4, 7) P(5 ,8–10, 14-16, 18,22)	K(2) P(11)	K(2,4) P(2-5, 8, 15, 16)	K(3) P(4)
Professtional Development for School and District Staff	K(3, 5, 6) P(8, 9)	K(1, 2, 3, 5, 8) P(1–4, 7, 8, 10, 12, 17, 18)	K(4) P(3, 4,13, 14, 22)	P(16)	P(1, 11)	
Community Involvement and Collaboration	K(5) P(1, 2-7, 15, 18)	K(7, 8, 11) P(6, 7)	K(1) P(12)	K(1–5) P(1–3, 5–13)	K(3) P(6, 12)	
Organizational Resources and Operations	K(4, 5, 6) P(8, 10, 11, 13, 14)	K(6, 9–11) P(1, 2, 3, 5, 8, 9, 15, 16, 20)	K(1–8) P(3, 4, 6,–11, 12, 14–18, 20–23)	P(6, 7, 9, 12, 13)	P(3, 5, 8, 9, 11, 15, 16)	K(3) P(4)
School Board Relationships	K(2–6) P(8, 14)	K(7, 9) P(1, 4, 6)	K(1, 2, 4, 5, 7) P(3, 10, 12, 13, 16,17, 20, 22)	K(1, 2) P(2, 11)	K(2, 4) P(4, 5, 8, 10-13, 15)	K(1, 4, 7) P(3, 4)
Understanding and Responding to the Larger Political Context	K(5) P(1, 4, 5)		K(7) P(13, 18)	K(2, 4, 5) P(1, 2)	K(1–4) P(2, 4, 7, 9, 10, 12, 15, 16)	K(4, 5, 7, 8) P(1–5)

NOTE: k refers to **knowledge** indicator, p refers to **performance** indicator, and the number following each k or p represents the number of the indicator. There are no **disposition** indicators because the assessment is not designed to address dispositions.

All of the six ISLLC Standards were linked to five of the nine job categories. The remaining four categories were each linked to five of the six ISLLC Standards. In addition, most of the linkages were secured to multiple performance indicators and/or multiple knowledge indicators. This network of linkages supports the functional relationship between the job analysis categories and the ISLLC Standards.

APPENDIX D

---

*Correlation of ISLLC Standards with the Technology Standards
for School Administrators*

"There is clear and critical evidence of the key role leadership plays in successful school reform" (www.iste.org). The Collaborative for Technology Standards for School Administrators (TSSA Collaborative), in Draft (v2.2), has identified a common focus for how a school leader might enhance teaching, learning, and school operations through the use of technology.

The TSSA Standards were developed and reviewed nationally by a representative stakeholder group of PK-12 administrators. These standards describe what administrators should know and be able to do to optimize the use of technology in their schools. The standards present targets and are indicators of effective technology leadership in schools.

The TSSA Standards were designed to be applicable to the wide range of roles administrators play in schools, even when they may have the same title. Similar to the ISLLC Standards presented in this book herein, these standards must be used in a way that acknowledges the local context of school leadership. "Wise consumers of these standards and indicators must acknowledge a responsibility to apply this national resource appropriately within the local context. School and system size, degree of site-based governance, community characteristics, and strengths of individual administrators are but a few of the parameters that may cause variations in actual job roles" (www.iste.org).

These standards may be used for a variety of purposes just as the ISLLC Standards presented herein are used. Specifically, these standards can be applied in:

- Pre-service and in-service programs
- Role definition and job descriptions
- Self-assessment and goal setting
- Credentialing of administrators
- Accreditation of schools and administrator preparation programs

The technology standards are communicated as six standard statements with corresponding performance indicators for each. Three profiles of performance tasks are still under construction.

The information about the TSSA Standards that follows was originally produced as a project of the Technology Standards for School Administrators Collaborative. The chart on the next page is designed to show the correlation between the ISLLC Standards and these TSSA Standards.

CORRELATION OF ISLLC STANDARDS WITH THE
TECHNOLOGY STANDARDS FOR SCHOOL ADMINISTRATORS

STANDARDS	DESCRIPTION OF STANDARDS	COMPONENTS	TSSA STANDARDS DESCRIPTION
Correlation of ISLLC Standards for School Leaders with TSSA Collaboratives – Technology Standards for School Administrators			
STANDARD 1	A school administrator is an educational leader who promotes the success of all students by facilitating the development, articulation, implementation, and stewardship of a vision of learning this is shared and supported by the school community.	Leadership and Vision Assessment and Evaluation	**Leadership and Vision —** Educational leaders inspire the development of a shared vision for comprehensive integration of technology and foster an environment and culture conducive to the realization of that vision.
STANDARD 2	A school administrator is an educational leader who promotes the success of all students by advocating, nurturing, and sustaining a school culture and instructional program conducive to student learning and staff professional growth.	Learning and Teaching Productivity and Professional Practice	**Learning and Teaching —** Educational leaders ensure that curricular design, instructional strategies, and learning environments integrate appropriate technologies to maximize learning and teaching.
STANDARD 3	A school administrator is an educational leader who promotes the success of all students by ensuring management of the organization, operations, and resources for a safe, efficient, and effective learning environment.	Support Management Operations Productivity	**Productivity and Professional Practice —** Educational leaders apply technology to enhance their professional practice and to increase their own productivity and that of others.

STANDARDS	DESCRIPTION OF STANDARDS	COMPONENTS	TSSA STANDARDS DESCRIPTION
Correlation of ISLLC Standards for School Leaders with TSSA Collaboratives — Technology Standards for School Administrators			
STANDARD 4	A school administrator is an educational leader who promotes the success of all students by collaborating with families and community members, responding to diverse community interests and needs, and mobilizing community resources.	Professional Practice Productivity and Professional Practice	**Support, Management, and Operations** — Educational leaders provide direction to integrate technology tools into productive learning and administrative systems.
STANDARD 5	A school administrator is an educational leader who promotes the success of all students by acting with integrity, fairness, and in an ethical manner.	Social, Legal, and Ethical Issues	**Assessment and Evaluation** — Educational leaders use technology to facilitate a comprehensive system of effective assessment and evaluation.
STANDARD 6	A school administrator is an educational leader who promotes the success of all students by understanding, responding to, and influencingl the larger political, social, economic, legal, and cultural context.	Social, Legal, and Ethical Issues	**Social, Legal, and Ethical Issues** — Educational leaders understand the social, legal, and ethical issues related to technology and apply that understanding in practice.

REFERENCES

Beck, L. & Murphy, J. (1992). Searching for a Robust Understanding of the Principalship. *Educational Administration Quarterly*, 28, 387-96.

Bobbit, F. (1913). Some General Principles of Management Applied to the Problems of City School Systems. 12th Yearbook of the *National Society for the Study of Education, Part I, the Supervision of City Schools* (pp.7-96). Chicago: The University of Chicago Press.

Bulton, H. (1961). Public Schools: 1870-1850. (Unpublished doctoral dissertation) Washington University, 22.

Calkins, N. A. (1882). *School Supervision.* Providence, RI: Annenberg Institute for School Reform Corporation (pp. 498-499).

Council of Chief State School Officers. (1996). *Interstate School Leaders Licensure Consortium Standards for School Leaders.* Washington, DC.

Cubberley, E. P. (1916). *Public School Administration.* Boston: Houghton Mifflin.

Danielson, C. (1996). *Enhancing Professional Practice: A Framework for Teaching.* Alexandria, VA: Association for Supervision and Curriculum Development.

Dewey, J. (1916). *Democracy and Education.* New York: Macmillan.

Elmore, R. (2000). *Building a New Structure for School Leadership.* Washington, DC: The Albert Shanker Institute.

Evans, R. (1999). *Principals in the Line of Fire; Challenges of Authentic Leadership.* Providence, RI. The Annenberg Institute for School Reform.

Firth, G. R. & Pajak, E. F. (Eds.). (1998). *Handbook of Research on School Supervision.* New York: Simon and Schuster, Macmillan.

Fisher, J. C., Gorton, R. A., & Schneider, G. T. (1988). *Encyclopedia of School Administration and Supervision.* Phoenix, AZ: Oryn Press.

Fullan, M. (1991). *What's Worth Fighting for in the Principalship?* San Francisco: Jossey-Bass, Inc.

Glanz, J. (1976). Bureaucracy and Professionalism: A Historical Interpretation of Public School Supervision, 1875-1937. (Unpublished doctoral dissertation) in *Handbook of Research on School Supervision.* New York: Macmillan Publishing.

Glanz, J. (1998) Histories, Antecedent and Legacies of School Supervision. *Handbook of Research on School Supervision.* New York: Macmillan Publishing.

Harris, W. T. (1892). City School Supervision. *Educational Review*, 167-172.

Hoachlander, G., Alt, M. & Beltranena, R. (2001). *Leading School Improvement: What Research Says, A Review of the Literature.* Berkeley, CA: MPR Associates Inc.

Holloway, J, & Pearlman, M. (January, 2001). Reform Through Standards: The Ultimate Challenge. *Principal Leadership.* 1(5). Reston, VA: National Association of Secondary Principals. 40-44.

Institute for Educational Leadership. October 2000. *Leadership for Student Learning: Reinventing the Principalship.* Washington, DC: IEL.

Latham, A. & Holloway J. (1999). *The Profession of School Superintendent: An Analysis of the Responsibilities And Knowledge Areas Important For Beginning School Superintendents.* Princeton, NJ: Educational Testing Service.

Murphy, J. (1998 August). Preparation for the School Principalship: The United States' Story. *School Leadership and Management,* L18 (3), 359-373.

National Policy Board of Education Administration. Available on line at www.npbea.org/projects. Arlington, VA: NPBEA.

National Staff Development Council. (December 2000). *Learning to Lead, Leading to Learn: Improving School Quality Through Principal Professional Development.* Oxford, OH: National Staff Development Council.

Neuman, M. H. & Pelchat, J. A. (Producers). *Principals in the Line of Fire: The Challenges of Authentic Leadership* {Videotape}. Providence, RI: The Annenberg Institute for School Reform.

Saranson, S. (1971). *The Culture of the School and the Problem of Change.* Boston: Allyn and Bacon.

Sergiovanni, T. (1992). *Moral Leadership.* San Francisco: Jossey-Bass, Inc.

Spears, J. (1976). *Improving the Supervision of Instruction.* Englewood Cliffs, NJ: Prentice Hall.

Tannenbaum, R. (1996). *The Profession of School Administrator: An Analysis of the Responsibilities And Knowledge Areas Important For Beginning School Administrators.* Princeton, NJ: Educational Testing Service.

Taylor, F. W. (1911). *The Principals of Scientific Management.* New York: Harper and Brothers.

Van Meter, E. J. & McMinn C. (2001). Measuring a Leader. *Journal of Staff Development.* Oxford, OH: National Staff Development Council. 22:1. 32-35.

Zemelman, S., Daniels, H. & Hyde, A. (1998). *Best Practice: New Standards for Teaching and Learning in America's Schools* (2nd ed.). Portsmouth: Heinemann.

Notes

Notes

Notes

Notes

Notes

Notes

Notes

Notes